Effective Altruism and the Human Mind

Effective Altruism and the Human Mind

The Clash Between Impact and Intuition

STEFAN SCHUBERT
LUCIUS CAVIOLA

Oxford University Press is a department of the University of Oxford. It furthers
the University's objective of excellence in research, scholarship, and education
by publishing worldwide. Oxford is a registered trade mark of Oxford University
Press in the UK and certain other countries.

Published in the United States of America by Oxford University Press
198 Madison Avenue, New York, NY 10016, United States of America.

© Oxford University Press 2024

Some rights reserved. No part of this publication may be reproduced, stored in
a retrieval system, or transmitted, in any form or by any means, for commercial purposes,
without the prior permission in writing of Oxford University Press, or as expressly
permitted by law, by licence or under terms agreed with the appropriate
reprographics rights organization.

This is an open access publication, available online and distributed under the terms of a
Creative Commons Attribution – Non Commercial – No Derivatives 4.0
International licence (CC BY-NC-ND 4.0), a copy of which is available at
http://creativecommons.org/licenses/by-nc-nd/4.0/.

You must not circulate this work in any other form
and you must impose this same condition on any acquirer.

Library of Congress Cataloging-in-Publication Data
Names: Schubert, Stefan (Editor), editor. | Caviola, Lucius, editor.
Title: Effective altruism and the human mind : the clash between impact and intuition /
[edited by] Stefan Schubert and Lucius Caviola.
Description: New York, NY : Oxford University Press, [2024] |
Includes bibliographical references and index.
Identifiers: LCCN 2024006277 (print) | LCCN 2024006278 (ebook) |
ISBN 9780197757376 (paperback) | ISBN 9780197757390 (epub) | ISBN 9780197757406
Subjects: LCSH: Altruism. | Helping behavior.
Classification: LCC BF637.H4 E34 2024 (print) | LCC BF637.H4 (ebook) |
DDC 155.2/32—dc23/eng/20240308
LC record available at https://lccn.loc.gov/2024006277
LC ebook record available at https://lccn.loc.gov/2024006278

DOI: 10.1093/oso/9780197757376.001.0001

Printed by Marquis Book Printing, Canada

Contents

Introduction   1

PART I. OBSTACLES

1. The Norms of Giving   11
2. Neglecting the Stakes   30
3. Distant Causes and Nearsighted Feelings   44
4. Tough Prioritizing   61
5. Misconceptions About Effectiveness   76

PART II. INTERVENTIONS

6. Information, Nudges, and Incentives   101
7. Finding the Enthusiasts   120
8. Fundamental Value Change   135
9. Effective Altruism for Mortals   149

Acknowledgments   171
Index   173

Introduction

Humans are more altruistic than one might think. Many of us want to have a positive impact on the world. We donate to charity, volunteer for a good cause, or choose a career to make a difference. Annual US donations sum to $500 billion—about 2% of gross domestic product—and no less than 23% of Americans volunteer for a good cause (Lilly Family School of Philanthropy, 2023; United Census Bureau, 2023). People make real altruistic sacrifices on a scale that's often underappreciated.

But, unfortunately, much of our help isn't as effective as it could be. In this book, the effectiveness of your help is defined by how many lives you save or how much good you otherwise do with a given amount of resources. And, as we will see, many altruistic contributions aren't effective in this sense. For example, most donations don't go to the most effective charities—even though they can be at least 100 times more effective than the average charity, according to expert surveys (Caviola et al., 2020). (Throughout this book, we use the word *charities* in an expansive sense that includes what are sometimes called *nonprofits*.) This means that almost all the impact those donations could have had is lost. Much the same is true of other acts of altruism, like volunteering or socially motivated career choice (80,000 Hours, n.d.; Todd, 2020).

The fact that our altruistic efforts aren't more effective is surprising. In other domains of life, people are more focused on effectiveness. For instance, we are relatively good at getting value for money as consumers and investors. When we buy a new phone or invest our money in stocks, we try to get the most bang for our buck. We rarely forgo the chance of getting something that is 100 times more value for money. We would be bewildered if we found out that somebody chose to buy a new smartphone for $100,000 instead of $1000. But we take a different approach when we seek to help others and improve the world.

Only relatively recently did some people start to think more systematically about how we can apply evidence-based and effectiveness-oriented reasoning to altruism. A new philosophy and growing movement called *effective altruism* emerged around 2010. Effective altruism is, as the name suggests, about using the time, money, and other resources we allocate to others as effectively as possible.

On the face of it, effective altruism may seem like an obvious idea. So why is it still a relatively niche way of thinking? Why are most of us not particularly effective when we're helping others? And what can be done to change it? Those are the questions we try to answer in this book.

The Psychological Study of Effective Altruism

Most of the existing research on the psychology of altruism focuses on the amount of altruism: how much people give to others and how we can make them give more (Bekkers & Wiepking, 2011). By contrast, in this book, we rather focus on the effectiveness of people's altruistic efforts (Berman & Silver, 2022; Caviola et al., 2021; Erlandsson, 2020; Jaeger & van Vugt, 2022). This is a relatively neglected topic in the behavioral sciences—and yet it is, in our view, profoundly important.

First, it is theoretically important since it can illuminate the nature of human altruism. On the one hand, people sacrifice substantial resources for others, but on the other hand, they don't spend them effectively. Why is that? It's a pattern that challenges much of our conventional thinking about helping behavior. A thoroughly cynical theory couldn't explain the level of altruism, whereas a thoroughly idealistic theory couldn't explain the lack of impact. In the first part of the book, we try to explain why most people who choose to help aren't as effective as they could be.

Second, effective altruism is practically important. If people started to do good more effectively, many lives would be saved, and we could make more progress on some of the biggest global problems. In fact, we believe that increasing the effectiveness of people's help is more important than increasing the amount of resources (e.g., in the form of money or time) they allocate to others. As we've seen, the most effective ways of helping others can be at least 100 times more impactful than most alternative approaches, according to expert surveys (Caviola et al., 2020). If someone switches to one of these highly effective approaches, their impact will increase hugely. By contrast, it's hard to encourage people to increase the amounts that they give to others very substantially. For instance, convincing them to double their donations would typically be a tall order, and yet that would "only" double their impact—much less than we can achieve by increasing their effectiveness. Therefore, behavioral scientists should devote much more attention to increasing the effectiveness of people's help. In the second part of the book, we show how that can be done, drawing on the psychological explanation from the first part of the book.

Effective Altruism as a Normative Framework

This book is written from the perspective that effective altruism is a desirable goal. We contrast the ideal of effective altruism with actual human psychology. That is, we look at how the descriptive (human psychology) deviates from the normative (the ideal of effective altruism). As our subtitle says, there is a clash between intuition and impact.

In many cases, it seems relatively uncontroversial that it is better to be more effective, in the sense we use the term here. For instance, most people agree that, everything else being equal, it is better to save two lives than one. But in other cases, it is not as uncontroversial. As we will see in Chapter 3, it tends to be more effective for people in rich countries to help people in distant developing countries than to help their compatriots. We think that, to the extent this is true, one should prioritize helping people in distant developing countries; but we realize that not everyone agrees. However, we hope that even readers who disagree with this view will find this book of interest as it explains why people don't always choose the most effective ways of helping others—regardless of whether that is desirable. We will discuss effective altruism's ethical standpoints and its definition of effectiveness in more detail in Chapter 5.

There Are Many Ways to Practice Effective Altruism

To maximize their positive impact, effective altruists tend to work on pressing global problems such as global poverty and health, animal welfare, and risks that threaten to cause human extinction (Todd, 2021). There are many strategies that one can employ to make progress on these problems. One strategy is to work on one of these problems directly, in your professional job. Another strategy is to give financial support to organizations working on these problems. A third is to conduct research to figure out new ways of having a large positive impact. A fourth is to engage in political advocacy. And there are still other strategies, as we will see in Chapter 9.

The goal of this book is to understand the psychology of effective altruism in general. We are interested in fundamental psychological obstacles to effective altruism, such as insensitivity to the scale of the opportunities we're given (Chapter 2) and partiality in favor of people close to us (Chapter 3). Many of the studies on effective altruism focus on charitable giving—mainly because it is simply easier to study one-off donation decisions than to study, for example, how an altruistic career unfolds over many years. Our exposition reflects that fact and covers many donation studies. However, this doesn't mean that charitable giving is the only way of practicing effective altruism—far from it. Effective altruism is, in principle, neutral about what strategies to use and, in fact, uses many different strategies (Chapter 9).

We should also make clear that since we focus on the psychology of effective altruism, we will only briefly cover how to practice effective altruism (in Chapter 9). We don't assume any knowledge of effective altruism, but interested readers may want to look at introductions to effective altruism, such as William MacAskill's *Doing Good Better* (2015), Peter Singer's *The Most Good You Can Do* (2015), or The Centre for Effective Altruism's (2023) *Introduction to effective altruism program syllabus*.

Outline

In the first half of the book, we explain why most people aren't as effective as they could be in their altruistic endeavors. We identify a number of psychological obstacles to effective altruism.

In Chapter 1, we show that people tend to help others based on their feelings. Most people prioritize causes they find personally meaningful even if they learn that other causes are more effective. Moreover, this is propped up by widely shared norms. In most people's view, do-gooders are not obligated to prioritize the most effective causes. Charity and related forms of do-gooding are viewed as subjective domains, where we can freely choose between a wide range of options. These views are a root cause of why people's help to others isn't more effective.

In Chapter 2, we show that the differences in effectiveness between different charities are vast and that most people underestimate these differences. Accordingly, they also underestimate the importance of choosing the most effective charities. But while teaching people about these differences makes them more inclined to donate effectively, the effect is smaller than one might think. People exhibit *scope neglect*: They are insensitive to the scope or scale of altruistic opportunities. That reduces their urge to support the most effective causes, even if they learn that they are vastly much more effective than the alternatives.

In Chapter 3, we show that most people's altruism is *nearsighted*: It focuses on beneficiaries who are close to them. We can often be more effective by supporting beneficiaries who are distant from us in terms of space (e.g., people in distant developing countries), time (i.e., future people), and biology (i.e., animals); but we rarely do that. Our altruistic feelings evolved to facilitate cooperation among small groups of people, not to help distant strangers.

In Chapter 4, we show that people are reluctant to prioritize some ways of helping others over alternative approaches. To be effective, we must deprioritize less effective causes, even if they feel worthy of support—as any resources that we spend on less effective causes could have done more good if we had spent them on more effective causes. But most people find that unfair or otherwise objectionable. This aversion to prioritization is another important obstacle to effective altruism.

In Chapter 5, we show that another reason that people's help to others is often less effective than it could be is that they have many misconceptions about effectiveness. For instance, many charitable donors incorrectly equate effectiveness with low overhead or administration costs. Similarly, many people underestimate the value of indirect do-gooding strategies. And many are overly skeptical about the feasibility of measuring and comparing different ways of doing good.

In the second part of the book, we discuss how to overcome these psychological obstacles to effective altruism.

In Chapter 6, we discuss a series of targeted and relatively tractable techniques aimed at increasing the effectiveness of people's help to others. They include simply providing people with information about how to help effectively, as well as behavioral techniques such as nudging and incentivization. An advantage of these techniques is that they can make people help more effectively even if they don't change their fundamental values and preferences.

In Chapter 7, we study individual differences in people's inclinations toward effective altruism. We show that even though most people don't agree with all aspects of effective altruism, there are some people who do. We demonstrate that effective altruism's moral outlook consists of two psychological factors. First, there is *expansive altruism*—to be willing to help others, whether they are close to us or more distant. Second, there is *effectiveness-focus*—to be willing to choose the most effective ways of helping others. Only a few people are attracted to both expansive altruism and effectiveness-focus, and effective altruist outreach may be well advised to initially target them.

In Chapter 8, we turn to a more ambitious strategy. Can people's fundamental attitudes to doing good be changed? We review research on the effects of rational moral arguments on people's values and behavior and conclude that such arguments likely don't persuade everyone. However, they may persuade those who already are positively disposed toward effective altruism, whom we discussed in Chapter 7. Moreover, once they are onboard with effective altruism, social norms may gradually shift, which in turn may make broader groups want to join.

In Chapter 9, we discuss how to apply effective altruism in your own life. We show that when you practice effective altruism, you need to take your psychological limitations into account. For instance, while working all the time may seem effective, it risks leading to burnout—which would actually reduce your effectiveness. In order to do the most good, we thus need to acquire habits that are psychologically sustainable. We also discuss a number of high-impact causes that are popular in the effective altruism community, along with effective strategies for addressing those causes. We conclude by discussing avenues for future research.

References

Bekkers, R., & Wiepking, P. (2011). A literature review of empirical studies of philanthropy. *Nonprofit and Voluntary Sector Quarterly*, 40(5), 924–973.

Berman, J. Z., & Silver, I. (2022). Prosocial behavior and reputation: When does doing good lead to looking good? *Current Opinion in Psychology*, 43, 102–107.

Caviola, L., Schubert, S., & Greene, J. D. (2021). The psychology of (in)effective altruism. *Trends in Cognitive Sciences*, 25(7), 596–607.

Caviola, L., Schubert, S., Teperman, E., Moss, D., Greenberg, S., & Faber, N. S. (2020). Donors vastly underestimate differences in charities' effectiveness. *Judgment and Decision Making*, 15(4), 509–516.

80,000 Hours. (n.d.). *Career planning series: how to plan your high-impact career*. https://80000hours.org/career-planning/process/. Retrieved January 27, 2024.

Erlandsson, A. (2020). Hjälpdilemman: Beslutsfattande när man inte kan hjälpa alla i nöd [Helping dilemmas: Decision-making when one cannot help everyone in need]. *Statsvetenskaplig Tidskrift, 122*(4), 601–624. Available in English on PsyArXiv.

Jaeger, B., & van Vugt, M. (2022). Psychological barriers to effective altruism: An evolutionary perspective. *Current Opinion in Psychology, 44*, 130–134.

Lilly Family School of Philanthropy. (2023, June 20). *Giving USA: Total U.S. charitable giving declined in 2022 to $499.33 billion following two years of record generosity*. https://philanthropy.iupui.edu/news-events/news/_news/2023/giving-usa-total-us-charitable-giving-declined-in-2022-to-49933-billion-following-two-years-of-record-generosity.html

MacAskill, W. (2015). *Doing good better: Effective altruism and a radical new way to make a difference*. Guardian Faber Publishing.

Singer, P. (2015). *The most good you can do: How effective altruism is changing ideas about living ethically*. Yale University Press.

The Centre for Effective Altruism. (2023, October). *Introduction to effective altruism program syllabus*. https://docs.google.com/document/d/1ju83W3yFqvUBvsSrHadjEwazNBphCTmLWd-xZkVArBM/edit. Retrieved January 27, 2024.

Todd, B. (2020, December). *Where's the best place to volunteer?* 80,000 Hours. https://80000hours.org/articles/volunteering/. Retrieved January 27, 2024.

Todd, B. (2021, August 9). *How are resources in effective altruism allocated across issues?* 80,000 Hours. https://80000hours.org/2021/08/effective-altruism-allocation-resources-cause-areas/. Retrieved January 27, 2024.

United Census Bureau (2023, January 25). *At Height of Pandemic, More Than Half of People Age 16 and Over Helped Neighbors, 23% Formally Volunteered*. https://www.census.gov/library/stories/2023/01/volunteering-and-civic-life-in-america.html

PART I
OBSTACLES

1
The Norms of Giving

Every day, we face vast numbers of decisions ranging from the small and trivial to the large and consequential. What restaurant should we choose? Should we go home by car or train? How to save for retirement? What medical treatment should I get?

We tend to take very different approaches depending on the nature of the decision. For instance, when we decide what restaurant to go to, we typically take a *subjective approach* based on our own feelings and tastes. We listen to others' recommendations, but we're not prepared to let objective data and metrics trump our preferences. Restaurant choice is seen as a subjective matter where there is no right or wrong. While there is some scope for expertise, it is limited. At the end of the day, we know our own preferences best.

For a very different kind of decision, consider investments in retirement savings. Most people take an *objective approach*—based on data, metrics, and expert advice—to such decisions. Though they may have favorite companies and ways of saving, they often change their minds if experts say that other strategies yield higher returns. After all, the purpose of saving for retirement is to maximize your pension. In that sense, there are objectively right and wrong answers to the question of how to invest. And the experts are more likely to know the correct answer than most savers are. Therefore, it makes sense to defer to them.

But how do we make decisions when we are trying to do good in the world? Do we take the subjective approach we often use when deciding on a restaurant? Or the objective approach that we tend to use for retirement investment decisions?

In an instructive survey, Jonathan Berman and his colleagues (2018) studied that question. They presented participants with a number of decisions and asked what criteria they would use. Would they choose based on personal feelings and taste or objective quality and effectiveness metrics?

As expected, most participants said they would use subjective criteria when deciding on a restaurant. The same was true of purchases of art. By contrast, most participants said they would use objective criteria for decisions about investments, medical treatments, and cell phone purchases. But how did they think about charitable giving decisions?

At first glance, one might think that people would use objective criteria for charitable giving decisions. They have many similarities with investment decisions, for which we use objective criteria. Both investments and donations involve allocating money toward some enterprise (a for-profit company and a charity, respectively). We typically implement both sets of decisions via an online interface. And we expect a certain output, both as investors and as donors. Investors expect to receive financial returns, whereas donors expect to see improvements in the social issue in question.

But there the similarities end. Even though investments and donations have similar decision-making structures, Berman and his colleagues (2018) found that most people don't use the objective approach that they use for investments when they make decisions about charitable donations. Instead, they use the more intuitive approach that they use when deciding on a restaurant or a piece of art. Berman and his colleagues show that, for most people, decisions about charitable donations are based on subjective preferences, rather than on objective effectiveness metrics. They are about expressing ourselves and our personal feelings and values. If a charity feels right, then most people go for it, even if its impact is limited. That attitude stands in stark contrast to how they view their investments, where the bottom line is what ultimately counts.

In another study, Berman and his colleagues (2018) provided more direct evidence that donors let feelings trump effectiveness. Participants were told that they could support three different kinds of medical research: research on arthritis, heart disease, or cancer. They were also told that independent evaluators had rated arthritis research to be the most effective kind of research, that heart disease research was number two, and that cancer research was the least effective. However, participants' donation preferences had a completely reversed order: Most people said they would donate to cancer research, heart disease research was second most popular, and only a small minority preferred donating to arthritis research. This is probably at least in part because this reverse order matches people's feelings. Most people likely feel more strongly about cancer research than about research on heart disease or arthritis. Such feelings for particular causes override information about effectiveness.

Personal Connections

Thus, people feel more for some ways of doing good and often pursue them even when they are informed that other options are much more effective (Andreoni, 1990; Bloom, 2017). But this raises the question of what causes people to feel more for some ways of doing good than for others. What ways of doing good do people feel particularly strongly for and why? Where do these feelings come from?

A key source of altruistic preferences is personal connections (Small & Simonsohn, 2008). People often experience a personal connection with a specific cause. That could partially explain why most people prefer giving to cancer research over giving to arthritis research. Many have relatives and friends who died of cancer, and thus may feel personally vested in fighting it. By contrast, arthritis is a less salient disease, which people are less likely to feel personally connected with.

Personal connections may also be part of why Western donors prioritize giving to charities fighting diseases that are common in the West, such as cancer, over charities that fight diseases that disproportionately affect the global poor, such as malaria. As we will see in Chapter 9, several of the most effective charities in the world are devoted to fighting malaria and other medical conditions common in developing countries. Still, many donors prefer giving to cancer charities that don't have the same evidence of effectiveness.

Another example relates to charities helping animals (see Chapter 3). Many people have a personal connection with dogs, cats, and other pets. By contrast, fewer people have personal connections with farmed animals such as cows, pigs, and chickens. This is likely part of the reason many people prioritize pets over farmed animals. In a study, Lucius Caviola and his collaborators Jim Everett and Nadira Faber (2019) found that participants who were asked to allocate $100 between a charity that helps dogs and a charity that helps pigs on average gave $69 to the former and only $31 to the latter. This is matched by real-world donation behavior. Donors tend to prioritize animal shelters and other charities helping pets over charities that advance the welfare of animals living at factory farms. Animal Charity Evaluators (2024), which rates the effectiveness of charities helping animals, estimates that 95% of US donations to charities helping animals are directed to companion animal organizations, whereas only 3% are directed to charities focused on helping farmed animals. And yet charities that improve the appalling conditions at factory farms (e.g., through corporate campaigns) can often be remarkably effective. Animal Charity Evaluators and

Founders Pledge (another effective altruism-aligned research organization) recommend several such charities, including Compassion in World Farming USA and The Humane League (Animal Charity Evaluators, n.d.; Clare, 2023). By contrast, they don't recommend any charities supporting pets.

As we can see, personal connections and experiences play a central role when people select altruistic causes (Effective Altruism Forum, n.d.). Effective altruism emphasizes the importance of cause-neutrality: that we should not prejudge which cause to focus on—be it climate change, wildlife conservation, homelessness, or something else. Instead, cause-neutrality dictates that we should compare the effectiveness of different causes and choose the one that saves the most lives or otherwise does the most good. But our intuitions typically aren't cause-neutral. Many decide on a cause prior to having made any effectiveness comparisons. And they often settle on a cause because they have a personal connection with it.

But people's helping decisions are not just influenced by their own personal connections with a cause. They are also swayed to make donation decisions based on vicarious personal connections. People are more inclined to listen to fundraisers who have a personal connection with the cause that they champion. Campaigns that highlight fundraisers who identify with their cause have proved to be especially effective at increasing donations (Chapman et al., 2019). Such fundraisers are personally invested in their cause, and many people seem to like that attitude. People want charitable giving to be heartfelt and personal.

A special kind of personal connection is loyalty to the charity itself. In the 2015 *Money for Good* report, only 13% of the surveyed American donors said that they intended to donate to different charities next year (Camber Collective, 2015, p. 26). This is probably partly because donors develop a sense of loyalty to the charity itself (though other factors, such as sheer inertia, no doubt also contribute). They may feel that they would disappoint the charity they usually donate to if they stopped supporting them. That is particularly so since many fundraisers contact donors directly and build personal relationships with them.

Urgency

Just as we feel more for problems that we have a personal connection with, we also feel more for more problems that are more urgent. Suppose that you hear about two charities that you could donate to. One of them distributes medicines to people in dire need after an earthquake, whereas the other addresses recurring health problems such as parasitic worms. Which charity feels more emotionally engaging? And where would you donate to? In a study we conducted with Jason Nemirow, we found that people on average wanted to support the disaster relief charity (Caviola et al., 2020). Notably, that was not because they thought the disaster relief charity was more effective (they thought the two charities were roughly equally effective). Instead, the main reason was a preference for supporting the disaster relief charity that was independent of beliefs about effectiveness. (Though we also found that beliefs about effectiveness did influence decisions to support the disaster relief charity; see Chapter 6.) Disasters that suddenly appear are more emotionally salient than persistent or recurrent problems we have with us all the time. We grow accustomed to them, and that weakens our feelings.

A related reason that people focus on disasters is that our news sources concentrate so much on them. Big disasters often dominate headlines and are widely reported on in the media. Persistent problems, on the other hand, aren't considered "news" in the present media environment and so aren't reported on as much. And causes that get more media attention naturally receive more donations. This mechanism strengthens the bias in favor of disaster relief even further.

And yet, disaster relief usually isn't among the most effective ways of helping. GiveWell (2023), an effective altruism charity evaluator, rather recommends charities that work on persistent or recurrent problems, like vitamin A deficiency (Helen Keller International) and malaria mitigation (Against Malaria Foundation, Malaria Consortium). While these causes don't stir most donors' emotions as much as disaster relief charities do, they're likely more effective.

One reason disaster relief is less effective than one might have thought is that it's often very difficult to assist in time to save lives. In many cases, help must arrive very soon after the disaster struck to make a meaningful difference. More often than not, that's not logistically possible (Karnofsky, 2010).

The popularity of disaster relief also reduces its effectiveness. Since many people support disaster relief, it's usually not neglected. The most obvious opportunities to mitigate disasters are already taken, meaning additional contributions will be less effective. Instead, we should prioritize more neglected problems. That will often mean problems our psychological biases disfavor, such as persistent or recurring problems.

Failure to Research Effectiveness

We have seen that when we help others, we tend to take a subjective approach. We prioritize emotionally appealing interventions like cancer research even if we know that other interventions, such as arthritis research, are more effective. We make decisions based on our feelings, and if they clash with effectiveness, our feelings usually win.

And, de facto, our feelings often do clash with effectiveness. Unfortunately, the ways of helping that we feel most strongly about are rarely the ones that happen to be the most effective. Our feelings are not proxies for effectiveness and have not evolved for that purpose. We will see more examples of that in the coming chapters.

But the fact that our altruistic decision-making is based on subjective feelings also reduces effectiveness in another way. Because we don't think that we need to choose the most effective ways of helping others, we don't do the research that's necessary to find them. People who want to make decisions based on objective effectiveness information must put in a lot of research to find that information. That can be hard work. By contrast, if we go with what it feels like, then we don't need to do that work. Hence, the fact that people take a subjective approach to helping others makes them less inclined to study the effectiveness of different helping strategies.

The 2015 *Money for Good* report found that no more than 38% of surveyed American donors did any form of research before donating, and only 9% researched multiple different charities to compare them (Camber Collective, 2015, p. 26). Moreover, it's unclear how many of those are focused on effectiveness in the sense used in this book (Chapter 5). Thus, the fraction of donors who do sufficiently thorough research may be vanishingly small. Many make quick and spontaneous donation decisions, based on gut instincts. For example, they may donate on the spot to fundraisers without doing any checking at all. These attitudes contrast strongly with attitudes to investment and consumption decisions. We are less reflective and less effectiveness-minded when we donate to help others than when we spend money for our own benefit.

As a result of this lack of research, most people don't know what the most effective charities are. In another study we conducted with Jason Nemirow, we asked people to name a highly effective charity (Caviola et al., 2020). We found that almost no one (5 of 170 participants across two studies) named a charity identified as highly effective by expert researchers. Similarly, this lack of research leads people to have many sorts of misconceptions about how to donate effectively, as we will see in Chapter 5. All this reduces the effectiveness of their help further. Thus, the subjective approach that people take when they help others reduces effectiveness not only because it directly leads to them choosing less effective ways of helping but also because it leads them to do less research. Since they don't do the requisite research, they typically don't even know what the most effective ways of helping are.

The Norm of Emotional Helping

But it's not just that our help to others actually tends to be driven by feelings and preferences, rather than by objective information about effectiveness. Most people also find it justified to help in this way. It is the norm in our society.

Let us again look at the seminal paper by Berman and his colleagues (2018). In another study of charity choice, they asked the participants not which charity they would choose themselves but rather which charity a hypothetical donor, Mary, should choose. Should she donate to a more effective charity or a charity she feels more strongly for? Even though it clearly said that Mary could do more good if she donated to the more effective charity, most participants said that Mary should donate to the charity that speaks to her heart. People usually don't think that others need to use the most effective ways of helping. They don't criticize people who prioritize causes they care about over more effective alternatives. Instead, they expect others to give based on their feelings and personal preferences. Helping with our hearts is seen as good and appropriate. The norm is that our help should be based on our emotions, rather than on objective information about effectiveness.

And precisely for that reason, our helping norms don't require us to put a lot of research into charity effectiveness. If a charity speaks to our hearts, it's fine to donate to it, even if we haven't studied it extensively. We can even give spontaneously to a fundraiser in the streets if their message appeals to us. In the 2010 *Money for Good* report, one donor said that "giving to charity should be the easy thing in my life" (Hope Consulting, 2010, p. 38). In many ways, that statement encapsulates our norms about research on charity effectiveness.

But the norm that it is permissible to choose less effective ways of helping only applies to charitable donors, volunteers, and other people who aren't seen as responsible for outcomes. We have different norms for people who are in a position of responsibility. Another study from the paper by Berman and his colleagues (2018) illuminates this. They asked participants whether a charitable donor, on the one hand, and the president of a local medical research center, on the other, should prioritize cancer or arthritis research. In line with their other studies, most people thought that the donor should prioritize cancer research, the more emotionally appealing option. But in the case of the research center president—who is in a position of responsibility—the pattern was reversed. Most participants thought the research center president should prioritize arthritis research, the more effective option. Our norms for people in a position of responsibility (e.g., research center presidents, government officials, and medical doctors) thus seem to be quite different from our norms for donors. When you're put in charge of allocating limited financial resources or are making decisions on behalf of others, you cannot just go with your feelings. Instead, you're expected to choose the most effective option. Being in a position of responsibility thus appears to be more like being an investor than a charitable donor. In such contexts, we are supposed to go with objective information about effectiveness rather than subjective preferences and feelings.

These norms have tremendous importance because humans are a social, norm-following species (Bicchieri, 2005; Gross & Vostroknutov, 2022). How we are perceived by our peers matters hugely to us. We are much more likely to behave in a certain way if it strengthens our reputation. Conversely, we are much less likely to engage in a certain behavior if it harms our reputation. People in a position of responsibility of course also have feelings and preferences for particular interventions, just as charitable donors do. But because the norm is that they should prioritize the interventions that do best on objective metrics, they are more likely to refrain from acting on those feelings.

Thus, while feelings and preferences for particular interventions are part of the reason that people often help less effectively as donors and volunteers, they are not a sufficient cause. If the norm had been that donors and volunteers should put aside their feelings and preferences and choose the most effective interventions, then many people would likely have done so. But, in fact, our norms say that we are free to donate and volunteer in less effective ways. That is a key part of the explanation of why most such help isn't effective.

But it is important to be precise about the role of norms in this explanation. Some might think that our norms actively reward us for choosing less effective ways of helping and penalize us for being effective. That sounds quite cynical and would be a sad state of affairs. But in our view, that is usually not the case. Granted, some features associated with effective help (e.g., prioritizing distant strangers over friends and family) can lead to reputational penalties (see below on social incentives to help effectively; Everett et al., 2018; Law et al., 2022). However, in general, people have a positive view of effective help, even though that doesn't always translate into behavior (see below on aversion to waste). Moreover, as we've seen, people usually don't object to the choices of donors and volunteers. People who donate to an effective charity are thus seen as free to do so.

The main issue is therefore not that effectiveness is penalized (it usually isn't) but that we aren't given much active encouragement to help effectively. Because the rewards for helping effectively tend to be weak or nonexistent, we choose based on our feelings and preferences for particular interventions—and they tend to be more or less uncorrelated with effectiveness. Thus, the key problem is the relative absence of pro-effectiveness norms, not norms saying it is actively bad to help effectively.

In our view, this is a positive conclusion since at least people aren't actively opposed to the idea of helping effectively. At the same time, the norm that helping ought to be driven by feelings and preferences rather than objective effectiveness metrics seems to be relatively strong. And just like many other norms, it favors the status quo. Because we are norm-following, we tend to do what is socially approved, even in the face of good arguments suggesting a different course of action. There is a conformity bias, which makes it hard for new ideas to get a hearing (Asch, 1951, 1955; Bond, 2005). People look at new ideas with skepticism and stick to their old ways. This tendency has likely been to effective altruism's disadvantage so far.

But this is not to say that norms cannot change. Over the course of history, we have changed a myriad of norms, on everything from smoking to ethnic discrimination to recycling. Norms are sticky and slow-moving, but they are not immutable. And because norms play such a central role in the explanation of why most people help less effectively, changing norms may be a key intervention point (Frank, 2021). We will return to this issue in Chapter 8, where we argue that creating new norms supporting effective altruism could be a major lever of change.

Voluntary Help and Responsibility

To better understand our norms of helping, it is useful to look at the philosophical distinction between *obligatory* and *supererogatory* actions. Obligatory actions are actions we must undertake: It is wrong not to undertake them. For instance, in a famous essay, Peter Singer (1972) argued that it would be wrong not to save a drowning child if we could do so at no other cost than muddy clothes. Supererogatory actions, in turn, are actions that are morally good but not obligatory (Archer, 2018). Saving someone's life at great risk for yourself may be an example. Such actions are generally seen as going beyond the call of duty. We are to be praised if we undertake them but are not to be blamed if we don't.

Charitable giving and volunteering are usually viewed as supererogatory, according to most people's intuitions. For instance, donors are commended for their donations, but most people don't think that donating is strictly morally obligatory. We don't get severely blamed for not donating to charity.

This may help us explain why we don't have to help effectively in such contexts. Since it's not considered obligatory to help in the first place, people who do decide to help are viewed as free to help in any way they like. When there are no strong norms of whether to donate, there aren't any strong norms of where to donate either (Pummer, 2016, 2022).

In a series of studies, we set out to probe that hypothesis (Caviola & Schubert, 2020). In one study, we asked participants to imagine that they had received leaflets from two charities working to prevent children from contracting malaria. One of the charities was said to be 10 times more effective than the other one (which focused on saving children in a different town), meaning it could save 10 times more children with the same amount of money. We then asked two questions. First, would it be wrong not to donate at all (i.e., not to donate to either charity)? And, second, if you decided to donate, would it be wrong to donate to the less effective charity?

As expected, most people answered no to both questions. They didn't find it wrong not to donate, and they didn't find it wrong to give to the less effective charity if one decided to donate. That is in line with our hypothesis that most people don't consider it obligatory to help effectively in cases where they don't consider it obligatory to help in the first place.

To get a better understanding of the link between obligations to help and obligations to help effectively, we also asked another group of participants about their views of a case involving children drowning in a pond (inspired by Peter Singer's [1972] drowning child thought experiment). Again, the participants were given two options that differed in effectiveness. We said that they could either choose to save 10 children or one individual child but that they did not have time to save all 11 children. Neither option entailed any personal risk.

As expected, participants on average said that it is obligatory to intervene in this case: that one must try to save some children. And notably, the participants in this condition were more inclined to say that it is obligatory to help the larger group of children (i.e., to help effectively) than the participants in the donation condition were.

Our interpretation of this is that people directly faced with drowning children feel a strong sense of *responsibility for the outcome* (i.e., the children's well-being). They feel that they must do what they can to solve the problem since it's their personal responsibility. As a consequence, many believe that they have to help effectively. There is a marked contrast with how most donors feel. They don't feel responsible for outcomes, and neither see themselves as obligated to donate, nor as obligated to donate effectively if they do donate. (And even people who do feel obligated to donate tend to put less emphasis on effectiveness, in part because the effectiveness of a donation is less visible than its amount; see below on social incentives to help effectively.)

Responsibilities for outcomes can arise in several ways. As we've seen, people are often explicitly assigned responsibilities for outcomes (e.g., as part of their professional role; cf. the president of a medical research center). But responsibilities can also arise via the *situational context*. It is because of the situational context that we feel stronger responsibilities for children drowning in front of us than for children dying far away. But what exactly makes the difference? What features of a situation increase your felt responsibility for outcomes?

In our studies, we found that one feature is particularly predictive: the presence of other helpers (Caviola & Schubert, 2020). When there are other people around who also could provide help, we feel less obligated to provide help and less obligated to choose the most effective ways of helping. There's a diffusion of responsibility. We feel less responsible for suboptimal outcomes when there are others around. But when there is no one else present, there is no one else to blame; and that leads to a greater sense of personal responsibility for the outcome. This can help explain the difference between our attitudes to donations and saving drowning children, respectively. You're the only person who could help the drowning children, whereas you're not the only person who could donate to help children in distant countries. Other people could step in if you don't donate. That reduces our sense of personal responsibility, which in turn reduces both our sense that we're obligated to donate and our sense that we are obligated to choose the most effective charity. It's much less likely that other people could step in if we don't decide to act to save the drowning children. That makes us feel more responsible for outcomes, more inclined to step in to help, and more likely to help in the most effective way.

And it's not just the existence of other donors that diffuses responsibility in charity contexts. There's another relevant actor: the charity itself. Some donors may feel that it's the charity's responsibility to ensure that their help is effective. Recall the claim that "giving to charity should be the easy thing in my life" (Hope Consulting, 2010, p. 38). Unfortunately, this is a naive attitude since it's unlikely that charities will switch toward more effective causes and interventions unless donors incentivize them to do so. Nevertheless, this is another way in which diffusion of responsibility may contribute to a reduced focus on effectiveness among donors. Notice that there's a disanalogy with personal consumption, where there's no such diffusion of responsibility: It's clear that only the consumers themselves can ensure that their money is spent effectively. That is likely part of why consumer decisions tend to be more effectiveness-focused than donation decisions.

Are We Obligated to Donate Effectively?

While most people think that donors and volunteers don't have an obligation to help effectively, several philosophers in the effective altruism movement disagree with that view. In his "Famine, Affluence, and Morality," Peter Singer (1972) famously argued that there is no fundamental normative difference between physically saving the lives of children drowning in front of us and saving the lives of children far away with our donations. Though most people, including many philosophers, view these cases as normatively different, Singer (1972) argued that distance, urgency, and the presence of other helpers are all morally irrelevant (Kamm, 2008; Sterri & Moen, 2021; Temkin, 2022). Therefore, our obligations to donate to the global poor are just as strong as our obligations to save drowning children in front of us. Relatedly, our obligations to choose the most effective ways of helping the global poor are just as strong as our obligations to save the larger group of children.

Theron Pummer (2016, 2022) provides another argument for obligations to donate effectively. He rejects the link between obligations to provide help and obligations to provide that help effectively. Instead, he argues that even if it is not obligatory to donate to charity, it is obligatory to choose the most effective charities once we decide to donate. Donating to charity is a non-trivial sacrifice, and, depending on the circumstances (e.g., our wealth), it could be argued that we are not obligated to make such sacrifices. By contrast, prioritizing the most effective charities over the charities that we feel the most for is a much smaller sacrifice. At the same time, it greatly increases our help to the beneficiaries. Therefore, we are obligated to donate to the most effective charities if we decide to donate in the first place, Pummer argues. We may have a preference for a specific charity, but that preference cannot be given that much weight relative to the interests of the beneficiaries. In the words of Joe Horton (2017), it's "all or nothing." We can choose either not to donate ("nothing") or to give to an effective charity ("all"), but we cannot choose to give to a less effective charity.

Social Incentives to Help Effectively

These philosophical views notwithstanding, as a psychological matter, norms of helping others and norms of helping effectively are connected. It's seen as more obligatory to help effectively when it's seen as obligatory to help in the first place (e.g., when you're helping drowning children).

But there are also differences between norms of helping and norms of helping effectively. While it's usually not seen as obligatory to donate or volunteer, we will often be celebrated if we do so. If we sacrifice our resources for others, we will reap reputational benefits (Hardy & van Vugt, 2006). People like those who help others. Charitable giving and volunteering are promoted and seen as good things in society.

By contrast, decisions to help effectively are not nearly as celebrated. People evaluate donors and volunteers on the basis of how much they sacrifice and not on the basis of their impact (Berman & Silver, 2022). The focus is on the quantity of help, whereas the effectiveness is largely neglected.

Why is that? Why are people more focused on the quantity of someone's help than its effectiveness? In this chapter, we've so far focused on the contrast between people who have a position of responsibility and those who don't (the former typically need to be effective, the latter typically don't). We now turn to another contrast: that between the strong emphasis on the quantity of someone's help and the much weaker emphasis on effectiveness. Both contrasts can illuminate why people aren't more effective when they help others.

A popular explanation of the stronger emphasis on quantity focuses on evidence of character: on what we can infer from the quantity and the effectiveness, respectively, of someone's help (Burum et al., 2020; Jaeger & van Vugt, 2022; Miller, 2000; Simler & Hanson, 2017; Yoeli & Hoffman, 2022). In many situations, people will interpret a large donation or other altruistic sacrifice as relatively straightforward evidence of altruism—a positive character trait. Relatedly, it is evidence against them being selfish. Everything else being equal, we think that people who make such sacrifices are more altruistic and less selfish than those who don't. We can observe the size of someone's help and come to a rough agreement on how praiseworthy it was.

By contrast, it's often much less clear what to infer from the effectiveness, or lack thereof, of someone's help. When someone well off chooses not to give to charity, it can be natural to think it's because they're selfish. It's often harder to see why someone would give less effectively. If the relative levels of effectiveness of different charities are known (and there are no other relevant factors), someone prioritizing a less effective charity may appear more confusing than selfish. Accordingly, third parties may judge them less harshly.

And when a donor doesn't know the relative levels of effectiveness, them choosing a less effective charity is typically not strong evidence of their character either. Moreover, as Bethany Burum, Martin Nowak, and Moshe Hoffman (2020) point out, the fact that it is often difficult to observe the effectiveness of someone's help makes it hard to agree on how praiseworthy it was. That may undermine the development of pro-effectiveness norms.

Relatedly, a common belief is that if different ways of helping are different in nature, then we can't compare their relative impact. As we will see in Chapter 5, many view the relative impact of work on different causes (climate change vs. local homelessness, art museums vs. pandemics, etc.) as incomparable. By contrast, everyone realizes that it clearly is possible to compare how much people help: how many hours they put in or how many dollars they donate. This may partially explain why people focus on the quantity of help rather than on effectiveness when judging the helper's character.

Lastly, people prefer their family and friends to be naturally inclined to support them and may think that a deliberate, calculating approach to, for example, donations is evidence against that. They prefer if their friends don't constantly make cost–benefit analyses of whether it's worth it to stay friends with them and may suspect that someone who uses such methods with regard to donations also employs them with regard to personal relationships (Hoffman et al., 2015). One study found that people view empathetic donors, who donate with their heart, to be warmer and more trustworthy than calculating and deliberate donors, who use cost-effectiveness estimates to determine their donations (Montealegre et al., 2020). Similarly, as we saw, there is evidence that people who (e.g., for reasons of effectiveness) prioritize helping distant people over socially close people could suffer a reputational penalty (Everett et al., 2018; Law et al., 2022). Thus, while contributing resources to altruistic causes tends to be seen as evidence of good character, the reputational effects of using those resources effectively are more ambiguous.

Aversion to Waste

People don't think that it's obligatory to help effectively and often give to less effective charities even when they know that another charity is more effective. But that doesn't mean that they find effectiveness wholly unimportant. So far, we have focused on donation decisions involving groups of beneficiaries that don't overlap much (e.g., arthritis patients and cancer patients). In such cases, choosing the more effective option (i.e., arthritis) entails that members of the other group (i.e., cancer patients) will get deprioritized. As we will see in more detail in Chapter 4, people are averse to such deprioritization.

But there is another case, where choosing the more effective option doesn't entail that some people get deprioritized. The philosopher Derek Parfit (1982) created an illuminating thought experiment about such cases. Suppose that there is an accident and that a man is about to lose both arms. We could intervene (at some risk for ourselves), and if we do so, we could save either both of his arms or just one of them. Parfit argues that in such a case it would be "grossly perverse" to only save one arm (1982, p. 131). Saving both arms would benefit the man while not costing anyone else anything. If we decide to intervene, we should save both arms.

Another kind of situation is where we could save either the lives of a particular group of people or the lives of a larger group that includes the smaller group. Joe Horton (2017) has argued that if we decide to intervene in such a case, then we have an obligation to save the larger group. We ran a series of studies of such cases and found that most people consistently thought it would be wrong to choose the less effective option (Caviola & Schubert, 2020). They find it wrong to settle for saving a smaller group if we could save that group plus additional lives.

In these cases, choosing the more effective option is what economists call *Pareto-efficient*: a technical term that means that at least some people become better off, and no one becomes worse off. In other words, no one is deprioritized, unlike in the case involving arthritis and cancer patients. That means that choosing the less effective option is simply seen as wasteful: as squandering resources that could be used to help more people. We believe that people are averse to such waste and that this can partially explain why they dislike charities that are perceived as spending too much on overhead (Chapter 5). Likewise, some large donations to prestigious universities have met widespread resistance, which may in part be because they're seen as wasteful (Babbitt, 2022; Feloni, 2016). Thus, it is not true, as is sometimes said, that people are entirely uninterested in effectiveness. They very much do care about effectiveness. In the 2010 *Money for Good* surveys, 90% of donors said that effectiveness was one of their key criteria when choosing a charity, and 72% of donors thought that the charities they donate to are indeed effective (Hope Consulting, 2010, p. 18).

But while people do have a preference for effectiveness, they also have other preferences and values; and they often let them take precedence. Everything else being equal, people prefer the more effective ways of doing good—but in the real world, everything is typically not equal. In particular, different strategies for doing good almost always benefit different people. And in such situations, people don't necessarily choose the most effective approaches. Instead, their choices are often based on their personal connections or other criteria that are not good proxies for effectiveness. Thus, even though people do have a preference for effectiveness, that preference has a muted impact on their altruistic decisions.

Conclusion

When people are looking to help others, they are usually driven by their feelings. They don't find effectiveness wholly unimportant: On the contrary, they often mention that they want the charities to which they donate to be effective. But in practice, they tend to let their personal preferences take precedence. They choose causes that are particularly urgent or that they have a personal connection with rather than those that are most effective. And it is not just that they act this way; they also find it morally correct to do so. They find it justified. Most people don't think that we are obligated to choose the most effective ways of doing good. That is, in part, because they don't feel responsible for making sure that the problems they address are solved. They think that people can choose whatever way of helping they prefer, and as long as their contributions aren't directly wasteful, they're beyond reproach. Moreover, the quantity of someone's help is seen as stronger evidence of character than its effectiveness, leading to a focus on quantity at the expense of effectiveness.

References

Andreoni, J. (1990). Impure altruism and donations to public goods: A theory of warm-glow giving. *The Economic Journal of Nepal, 100*(401), 464–477.
Animal Charity Evaluators. (2024, January). *Why farmed animals?* Retrieved January 27, 2024 from https://animalcharityevaluators.org/donation-advice/why-farmed-animals/
Animal Charity Evaluators. (n.d.). Retrieved January 27, 2024 from *Recommended charities*. https://animalcharityevaluators.org/donation-advice/recommended-charities/
Archer, A. (2018). Supererogation. *Philosophy Compass, 13*(3), Article e12476.
Asch, S. (1951). Effects of group pressure on the modification and distortion of judgments. In H. Guetzkow (Ed.), *Groups, leadership and men* (pp. 177–190). Carnegie Press.
Asch, S. E. (1955). Opinions and social pressure. *Scientific American, 193*(5), 31–35.
Babbitt, A. (2022, March 17). Donating to Ivy League schools is ineffective and unnecessary, and it reinforces inequality. *Chronicle of Philanthropy*. https://www.philanthropy.com/article/donating-to-ivy-league-schools-is-ineffective-and-unnecessary-and-it-reinforces-inequality
Berman, J. Z., Barasch, A., Levine, E. E., & Small, D. A. (2018). Impediments to effective altruism: The role of subjective preferences in charitable giving. *Psychological Science, 29*(5), 834–844.
Berman, J. Z., & Silver, I. (2022). Prosocial behavior and reputation: When does doing good lead to looking good? *Current Opinion in Psychology, 43*, 102–107.
Bicchieri, C. (2005). *The grammar of society: The nature and dynamics of social norms*. Cambridge University Press.
Bloom, P. (2017). *Against empathy: The case for rational compassion*. Random House.
Bond, R. (2005). Group size and conformity. *Group Processes & Intergroup Relations, 8*(4), 331–354.

Burum, B., Nowak, M. A., & Hoffman, M. (2020). An evolutionary explanation for ineffective altruism. *Nature Human Behaviour, 4*(12), 1245–1257.

Camber Collective. (2015). *Money for good 2015*.

Caviola, L., Everett, J. A. C., & Faber, N. S. (2019). The moral standing of animals: Towards a psychology of speciesism. *Journal of Personality and Social Psychology, 116*(6), 1011–1029.

Caviola, L., & Schubert, S. (2020). *Is it obligatory to donate effectively? Judgments about the wrongness of donating ineffectively*. PsyArXiv Preprints. https://doi.org/10.31234/osf.io/j2h4r

Caviola, L., Schubert, S., & Nemirow, J. (2020). The many obstacles to effective giving. *Judgment and Decision Making, 15*(2), 159–172.

Chapman, C. M., Masser, B. M., & Louis, W. R. (2019). The champion effect in peer-to-peer giving: Successful campaigns highlight fundraisers more than causes. *Nonprofit and Voluntary Sector Quarterly, 48*(3), 572–592.

Clare, S. (2023, March 27). *Animal welfare report*. Founders Pledge. https://founderspledge.com/stories/animal-welfare-cause-report

Effective Altruism Forum. (n.d.) *Cause neutrality*. Retrieved January 27, 2024 from https://forum.effectivealtruism.org/topics/cause-neutrality.

Everett, J. A. C., Faber, N. S., Savulescu, J., & Crockett, M. J. (2018). The costs of being consequentialist: Social inference from instrumental harm and impartial beneficence. *Journal of Experimental Social Psychology, 79*, 200–216.

Feloni, R. (2016, August 17). Malcolm Gladwell says billionaires "sound like idiots" when they explain why they donate to large universities. *Business Insider*. https://www.businessinsider.com/malcolm-gladwell-billionaires-shouldnt-donate-to-large-universities-2016-8?r=US&IR=T

Frank, R. H. (2021). *Under the influence: Putting peer pressure to work*. Princeton University Press.

GiveWell. (2023, July). *GiveWell's top charities*. https://www.givewell.org/charities/top-charities. Retrieved January 14, 2024.

Gross, J., & Vostroknutov, A. (2022). Why do people follow social norms? *Current Opinion in Psychology, 44*, 1–6.

Hardy, C. L., & van Vugt, M. (2006). Nice guys finish first: The competitive altruism hypothesis. *Personality & Social Psychology Bulletin, 32*(10), 1402–1413.

Hoffman, M., Yoeli, E., & Nowak, M. A. (2015). Cooperate without looking: Why we care what people think and not just what they do. *Proceedings of the National Academy of Sciences of the United States of America, 112*(6), 1727–1732.

Hope Consulting. (2010, May). *Money for good: The US market for impact investments and charitable gifts from individual donors and investors*. https://search.issuelab.org/resource/money-for-good-the-us-market-for-impact-investments-and-charitable-gifts-from-individual-donors-and-investors.html

Horton, J. (2017). The all or nothing problem. *The Journal of Philosophy, 114*(2), 94–104.

Jaeger, B., & van Vugt, M. (2022). Psychological barriers to effective altruism: An evolutionary perspective. *Current Opinion in Psychology, 44*, 130–134.

Kamm, F. M. (2008). *Intricate ethics: Rights, responsibilities, and permissible harm*. Oxford University Press.

Karnofsky, H. (2010, March 11). The case against disaster relief. *The GiveWell Blog*. https://blog.givewell.org/2008/08/29/the-case-against-disaster-relief/. Retrieved January 27, 2024.

Law, K. F., Campbell, D., & Gaesser, B. (2022). Biased benevolence: The perceived morality of effective altruism across social distance. *Personality & Social Psychology Bulletin, 48*(3), 426–444.

Miller, G. (2000). *The mating mind*. Doubleday.

Montealegre, A., Bush, L., Moss, D., Pizarro, D., & Jimenez-Leal, W. (2020). *Does maximizing good make people look bad?* PsyArXiv Preprints. https://doi.org/10.31234/osf.io/2zbax

Parfit, D. (1982). Future generations: Further problems. *Philosophy & Public Affairs, 11*(2), 113–172.

Pummer, T. (2016). Whether and where to give. *Philosophy & Public Affairs, 44*(1), 77–95.

Pummer, T. (2022). *The rules of rescue: Cost, distance, and effective altruism*. Oxford University Press.

Simler, K., & Hanson, R. (2017). *The elephant in the brain: Hidden motives in everyday life*. Oxford University Press.

Singer, P. (1972). Famine, affluence, and morality. *Philosophy and Public Affairs, 1*(3), 229–243.

Small, D. A., & Simonsohn, U. (2008). Friends of victims: Personal experience and prosocial behavior. *The Journal of Consumer Research, 35*(3), 532–542.

Sterri, A. B., & Moen, O. M. (2021). The ethics of emergencies. *Philosophical Studies, 178*(8), 2621–2634.

Temkin, L. S. (2022). *Being good in a world of need*. Oxford University Press.

Yoeli, E., & Hoffman, M. (2022). *Hidden games: The surprising power of game theory to explain irrational human behavior*. Basic Books.

2
Neglecting the Stakes

Some companies are much more profitable than others. That's why investors spend a lot of time searching for the most promising companies. They want to ensure that they get the largest possible returns.

Similarly, some ways of doing good are much more effective than others. They save more lives, alleviate more suffering, or increase happiness more. That is a key premise of this book. If all ways of doing good were equally effective, there wouldn't be any point in searching for the most effective ones.

But how large are these differences? How effective are the most effective ways of doing good compared with the average way of doing good?

To keep things simple, let us focus on charities and specifically on charities that provide the world's poorest people with food, shelter, and basic health care. And let us measure effectiveness by the number of lives a charity saves with a given sum of money. (We discuss how to measure effectiveness more generally in Chapter 5.)

The magnitude of the differences in charity effectiveness of course matters a lot. If we don't do any research, we're unlikely to end up donating to one of the very best charities. Only by conducting careful research can we have any hope of finding them. Thus, the larger the difference between the most effective and the average charity is, the more valuable it is to research charity effectiveness.

Based on such reasoning, we ran a series of surveys of laypeople's and experts' beliefs about charity effectiveness together with our colleagues Elliot Teperman, David Moss, Spencer Greenberg, and Nadira Faber (Caviola et al., 2020). We first asked laypeople to estimate the difference in cost-effectiveness (defined in terms of lives saved per given amount of money) between a global poverty charity with the highest level of cost-effectiveness and a global poverty charity with an average level of cost-effectiveness. We posed this question in three different ways. In the *Tipping point* version, we asked how much money the average charity (*Charity B*) would need to save as many lives as the highly effective charity (*Charity A*) could save with $1000. In the *Explicit comparison* version, we simply asked "How many times more cost-effective

Effective Altruism and the Human Mind. Stefan Schubert and Lucius Caviola, Oxford University Press.
© Oxford University Press 2024. DOI: 10.1093/oso/9780197757376.003.0003

do you believe Charity A is in comparison to Charity B?" Finally, in the *Cost per life ratio* version, we asked how many dollars each charity would need to save one life. We then calculated what effectiveness ratio these estimates entailed.

We found broadly convergent results across these three versions of the question. In an online study, the *Tipping point* version yielded that the median participant thought that Charity A is 1.5 times more effective than Charity B, whereas the corresponding numbers for the *Explicit comparison* version and the *Cost per life ratio* version were 2.0 and 1.6 times. We also ran a study with students recruited on the University of Oxford campus, featuring only the *Tipping point* version. This time, the median estimate of the difference between the two charities was 2.0 times.

Overall, these results suggest that people believe that the most effective global poverty charities are 1.5–2 times more effective at saving lives than the average such charity. That's a substantial difference, implying that we could increase our impact by 50%–100% by researching charity effectiveness. But it also implies that even if we don't do any research and pick a charity randomly, we will, on average, retain much of our impact.

Next, we turned to experts on interventions helping the global poor, drawn from a range of universities and reputable organizations. For simplicity, we only asked them the most straightforward version of the question: the *Explicit comparison* version. We found that the experts' answers were markedly different. Whereas ordinary people thought that the most effective charities are 1.5–2 times more effective than the average charity, the average expert estimate was 100 times (Caviola et al., 2020)! And remember that these were all global poverty charities. Charities that work on entirely different causes—such as climate change, art, and local homelessness—are much more different, and therefore the differences in effectiveness between them could be even larger (Duda, 2023; Todd, 2023).

These expert estimates suggest that it's immensely valuable to research charity effectiveness. Not doing such research leads to huge losses of impact. If we pick a charity randomly instead of supporting the most effective charities, we could lose almost all of the impact we could have had. Thus, it's overwhelmingly important to prioritize the most effective charities: far more so than laypeople realize.

The fact that most people hugely underestimate the differences in charity effectiveness can help to explain why they aren't more inclined to give to the most effective charities and why they don't do more research to find them. In a follow-up study, we looked at the effects of informing people that the most effective charities are 100 times more effective than the average charity (according to expert estimates; Caviola et al., 2020). We asked participants how they would distribute $100 between a highly effective charity and a charity with an average level of effectiveness. Among participants who were not informed about the expert-estimated differences between charities, only 37% fully prioritized the highly effective charity, whereas the remaining 63% split their donation across the two charities. By contrast, among participants who were informed about the expert-estimated effectiveness differences, 56% gave exclusively to the highly effective charity, and only 44% split their donation.

The big differences in effectiveness likely extend beyond charity to other ways of helping, such as to career choice (Todd, 2023). These big differences in effectiveness are profoundly important and were a key rationale for the launch of the effective altruism movement. One of the pioneers of effective altruism, philosopher Toby Ord, wrote a seminal paper about these issues: "The Moral Imperative Toward Cost-Effectiveness in Global Health" (Ord, 2013). It's because some ways of doing good have so much greater impact than others that it is so important to pay attention to effectiveness.

Vast Differences and Heavy Tails

This raises two questions. First, why are some ways of doing good so much more effective than others? And second, why do people underestimate these differences in effectiveness? Let's focus on differences in charity effectiveness, which we understand best.

As we will see in Chapter 5, many people think that the key to charity effectiveness is the overhead ratio: the fraction of the budget that charities spend on things like administration and fundraising. In their view, the lower the overhead ratio, the more money goes to the charity's programs, and the more effective the charity is. And since overhead ratios probably only vary modestly between charities, the notion that effectiveness is identical to low overhead naturally leads to the conclusion that effectiveness differences also are modest.

But in fact, differences in effectiveness aren't primarily due to differences in overhead ratios. Overhead is largely unrelated to effectiveness since charities that pay high overhead often do so for good reason (see Chapter 5; Berrett,

2020). Instead, differences in effectiveness mostly stem from the problems charities choose to address and the methods they use to solve them. Some problems are much easier to make progress on, and charities that choose to focus on those problems are much more effective. Likewise, some methods allow us to make much more progress on a given problem, and charities that use those methods are much more effective.

Let's look at an example involving two different interventions addressing the same problem: blindness. There's an infectious disease affecting the eyelids called trachoma that can, if it's not treated, cause pain, visual impairment, and eventually blindness. It is unfortunately common in many countries in Africa, Asia, South and Central America, and the Pacific Islands. But the good news is that it's relatively cheap to address trachoma, using a range of measures, including hygiene improvement, antibiotics, and surgery. There is a lot of uncertainty about the precise level of cost-effectiveness, but experts have estimated that cataract surgery can reverse a severe visual impairment with $1000 (Hollander, 2017).

Another way to address blindness is via training guide dogs. That is, however, much more expensive. While it's impressive that it's possible to train a dog to guide a blind person, it's certainly not easy to do so. It takes a lot of time, and therefore costs a lot of money. Experts estimate it costs up to $50,000 to train a guide dog in the developed world (Guiding Eyes for the Blind, n.d.).

Thus, the reason charities that focus on trachoma prevention and treatment are so much more effective than charities that provide guide dogs isn't that they have lower overhead ratios. Instead, the reason is that they've chosen a method that's much more cost-effective: that can help many more people with the same amount of money.

This example is by no means unique. There are multiple global poverty interventions that are much more effective than most other interventions. But to see that, we need a more sophisticated metric for comparing health interventions. Health economists have developed such a metric: quality-adjusted life years (QALYs) per $1000 (Banerjee et al., 2011; Zeckhauser & Shepard, 1976). A QALY is a year of someone's life that is adjusted for its quality. For instance, a year spent suffering from a disease may only be seen as half as valuable as a year at full health, if people suffering from the disease find that it halves their subjective well-being. The QALYs/$1000 metric allows for comparisons of interventions that extend life with those that improve quality of life. For instance, according to this metric, curing someone from a disease that halves their quality of life is half as valuable as curing someone from a disease that otherwise would kill them, provided they go on to live the same number of years. In this example, the QALYs/$1000 metric suggests we should prioritize the life-improving cure if it's less than half as costly as the life-saving cure. We will introduce the QALYs/$1000 metric in more detail in Chapter 5.

Using the QALYs/$1000 metric, we can compare a wide range of global health interventions, such as different interventions to prevent and mitigate AIDS. These interventions vary substantially in cost-effectiveness. In a 2006 overview, it was estimated that combating AIDS via education of high-risk groups is no less than 1400 times more cost-effective than surgical treatment of Kaposi's sarcoma, a type of cancer associated with AIDS (Jamison et al., 2006; Ord, 2013). And once we move from comparing interventions addressing just one particular disease (such as AIDS) to comparing interventions addressing different diseases (such as malaria vs. AIDS), the differences in cost-effectiveness grow larger still. The most effective global health interventions, such as distribution of bed nets against malaria, was in this review estimated to be 15,000 times more cost-effective than the least effective global health interventions (Jamison et al., 2006; Ord, 2013).

Another important observation is that the number of interventions that reach the highest levels of effectiveness is small. If we order all global health interventions by their effectiveness, the result is a so-called heavy-tailed distribution (Figure 2.1). Most interventions have at most a moderate level of effectiveness, whereas a very small number of interventions are orders of magnitude more effective. This means that it can be hard to find the most effective interventions. We will discuss what methods effective altruist researchers use to identify them in Chapter 9.

Market Inefficiency

But the fact that some interventions are far more effective than others doesn't logically entail that some charities are far more effective than others. In principle, all charities could have employed the most effective interventions, like distribution of bed nets. Why don't they do that? There are plenty of remaining potential beneficiaries who could be helped cheaply through highly effective interventions. But most charities aren't taking those opportunities, instead choosing far less effective interventions. Why is that?

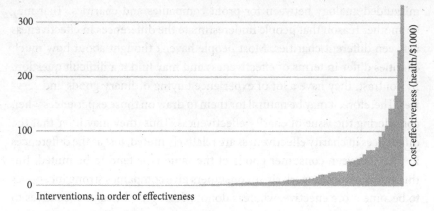

Figure 2.1 Cost-Effectiveness Distribution of Interventions in Global Health
Note: There are large differences in cost-effectiveness across health interventions. Most interventions have a modest level of effectiveness, but a small number are much more effective. Cost-effectiveness is here measured in disability-adjusted life years—another metric for comparing health interventions that measures years in perfect health lost—averted per $1000 (see Ord, 2013; Jamison et al., 2006). The figure is taken from (Duda, 2020). Reprinted with permission form 80,000 Hours.

The motivations of charities and their staff no doubt play a role, as does the wider discourse about charity in society. However, an underlying cause is that donors aren't focused on effectiveness. As we've seen, most donors don't use objective estimates of impact to decide where to give. That means that many donors give to charities with reduced effectiveness even if there are much more effective alternatives. Therefore, those charities will be able to continue to operate without needing to switch to the most effective causes and interventions. There is little market pressure toward effectiveness and efficiency.

The contrast to ordinary markets for consumer goods is striking. As we saw in Chapter 1, consumers are sensitive to differences in price and quality. If they learn that you can get some desirable product for a much lower price, they want to capitalize on that opportunity. They would tell their friends, who in turn would tell still more people, and so on. The rumor would spread like wildfire. Meanwhile, companies that demand a higher price for the same or a similar product would typically find it difficult to sell it. They would be forced to become more effective or be driven out of business. Through such mechanisms, prices for products of a specific type and quality typically converge to a relatively narrow range.

The "market" for charitable donations is thus profoundly different from the market for consumer goods. But even so, some people may make a misguided analogy between for-profit companies and charities. That may be another reason that people underestimate the differences in effectiveness between different charities. Most people haven't thought about how much charities differ in terms of effectiveness and may find it a difficult question. By contrast, they have a lot of experience buying ordinary goods and services. Therefore, it may be natural for them to draw on those experiences when considering the issue of charity effectiveness. Thus, they may infer that the differences in charity effectiveness are relatively muted, just as the differences in price between consumer goods of the same type tend to be muted. But this analogy doesn't work since consumers give companies strong incentives to become more effective, whereas donors don't give the same incentives to charities. Nevertheless, people may reason thus, meaning that misguided analogical reasoning may be part of the reason that people underestimate the differences in effectiveness between charities.

Insensitivity to Scale

We tend to decide how and whom to help based on our feelings. We've already seen several examples of how that makes our help less effective. It makes us choose ways of helping that are more urgent or that we have a stronger personal connection with, even when other ways of helping are more effective. But it also reduces effectiveness in another way. Our feelings (and associated thoughts) aren't sensitive to the large differences in effectiveness between different interventions. That, in turn, reduces our inclination to prioritize the most effective interventions—even when we learn the true size of the effectiveness differences.

It is true that informing people about the true differences in charity effectiveness makes people a bit more inclined to prioritize more effective charities. But this effect is not very large. Remember that in our study only 56% fully prioritized the highly effective charity even after learning that it's 100 times more effective than the average charity (Caviola et al., 2020). Moreover, information about differences in effectiveness doesn't seem to travel well. Even though it's been known for many years that some charities are much more effective than others, most donors haven't learned that. Donors certainly don't have the "can't wait to tell my friends" attitude that consumers and investors often have. Why aren't they more excited about opportunities to do 100 times more good? To help 100 times more people?

One reason is that we don't feel these differences in impact. We give with our hearts, but our feelings don't scale with the impact that we could have (Dickert et al., 2015; Slovic et al., 2007). We feel good about helping one person, but we don't feel twice as good about helping two. We certainly don't feel 10 times as good about helping 10 people or 100 times as good about helping 100 people.

In other words, we neglect the size or scope of the problem—what's been called *scope neglect* or *scope insensitivity*. Because of scope neglect, people don't reallocate their donations as much as one might have thought upon learning that some charities are massively more effective than others.

There is a range of studies on scope neglect, showing that our willingness to pay to solve a problem doesn't increase in proportion to the problem's size (Desvousges et al., 1993; Dickert et al., 2015; Slovic, 2007). In one study by Daniel Kahneman and Jack Knetsch (1992), participants were asked how much they would be willing to pay to clean up some polluted lakes. Two groups were told that the money would be used to clean up the polluted lakes in two different regions of Ontario, whereas a third group was told that it would be used for all polluted lakes in the entirety of Ontario. Despite Ontario being much larger than any of the regions that comprise it, the differences in willingness to donate were small.

We are often similarly insensitive to the size of humanitarian catastrophes. Two catastrophes that occurred in Pakistan and Haiti in 2010 provide an instructive example. Even though the catastrophe in Pakistan affected many more people (20 million vs. three million), donors contributed more ($3.1 billion vs. $2.1 billion) to Haiti, which experienced a smaller catastrophe (Dickert et al., 2015, p. 253; Global Humanitarian Assistance, 2012). While there could be confounding factors, the experimental evidence gives us reason to believe that scope neglect contributes to this kind of real-world difference in donation behavior.

At first glance, it may seem as if scope neglect shows that people's helping decisions are profoundly irrational. However, this isn't really fair. At least in part, scope neglect occurs because people are faced with a surprisingly hard problem. In most studies of scope neglect, different participants are given different opportunities to help, which they consider separately— in *separate evaluation*. Some participants are asked to donate to clear up a smaller number of lakes, whereas others are asked to donate to clear up a larger number of lakes. Moreover, they typically don't have any idea of what a normal or typical effort in the domain at hand would be. That means that they have no point of comparison to use to determine the size of a sensible donation (Hsee, 1996). As a result, their main donation criteria tend to be the type of harm and the type of beneficiary in the problem in question (e.g., pollution affecting people in Canada), while the number of beneficiaries has at best a muted effect (Baron & Greene, 1996).

However, things change when people are presented with several options side by side, in *joint evaluation* (Hsee, 1996; Kogut & Ritov, 2005b). In joint evaluation, people can compare different donation opportunities, and that makes them more sensitive to the size of the opportunities they are faced with. In other words, joint evaluation reduces scope neglect.

But in the real world, most decisions to help are made in separate evaluation, as it were. Most people tend to evaluate opportunities to help one by one, as they come. For instance, they rarely compare multiple different charities side by side to evaluate their relative effectiveness (Chapter 1). As a result, people are largely insensitive to the scope of the different opportunities to have an altruistic impact.

In part because of scope neglect, the huge differences in effectiveness between different ways of helping don't translate into huge differences in attention and support. Whether a charity can save one life or 100 lives with a given amount of money doesn't have the effect on donations one might have expected. Our feelings don't scale with the size of the opportunity, and since we tend to give with our hearts, neither do our donations.

"One Death Is a Tragedy, a Million Deaths Is a Statistic"

In fact, it's not just that our feelings don't scale with the numbers. In some cases, we may actually feel less for large groups of people than for individual victims.

People can feel extraordinarily strongly for particular suffering individuals, even when they don't know them. A prominent example is the case of "Baby Jessica," a girl who fell into a well in Texas in 1987. There was enormous media coverage and a huge outpouring of sympathy, leading to donations of more than $700,000 (Celizic, 2007). (Fortunately, Jessica was saved in the end without any major injuries.)

By contrast, there is often less media coverage of the much larger numbers of victims of malaria, schistosomiasis, and other diseases affecting the world's poorest people. And they receive much smaller donations than they need.

Some research suggests we have a tendency to prioritize individual, identifiable victims over larger numbers of non-identifiable or statistical victims: the so-called identifiable victim effect (Jenni & Loewenstein, 1997; Kogut & Ritov, 2005a; Small et al., 2007; Västfjäll et al., 2014). The idea is that when we see what the victim looks like and when we read about their history, we get a sense of who they are. They become more vivid for us as individuals—and that can trigger our empathy. By contrast, sheer statistical information about effectiveness is, according to this line of thinking, often insufficient to move us to donate. There's the brutal dictum that "one death is a tragedy, a million deaths is a statistic" (often attributed to Stalin, but it's unclear whether that's correct [Quote Investigator, 2010]). We should note, however, that several studies on the identifiable victim effect have not replicated and that we need more high-quality research on this topic (Hart et al., 2018; Maier et al., 2023; Majumder et al., 2022).

Every Life Matters Equally

From a normative perspective, most reasonable moral theories agree that it's untenable to prioritize identifiable victims over larger numbers of statistical victims. Statistical victims are also real people with real faces and real names, and there is no reason to believe that their fates are less pitiful. Similarly, it's untenable to value human lives less just because many lives have already been saved, as we effectively do when we exhibit scope neglect. The thousandth life we save is just as valuable as the first one. When we're considering the value of a human life, it's not relevant whether they are part of a big group or not. Our priorities should consistently mirror the numbers. The marginal value of saving a life doesn't diminish as we save more lives.

To some, this single-minded focus on the numbers seems cold: as if we're neglecting individuals in favor of abstract statistics. But nothing could be further from the truth. We want to save the greatest numbers precisely because individuals matter. The numbers are composed of individuals. These individuals become less salient to us when we're faced with large numbers because of the way our cognitive and emotional systems work. But that doesn't reduce their value in any way. Their value is independent of the quirks and idiosyncrasies of our thoughts and feelings. As Derek Parfit put it, "Why do we save the larger number? Because we *do* give equal weight to saving each.

Each counts for one. That is why more count for more" (1978, p. 301, emphasis in original).

On reflection, people tend to agree with that. We already saw that scope neglect is reduced under joint evaluation, when people can compare the different helping opportunities more easily. Furthermore, in one study, Stephan Dickert and his colleagues (2015) asked participants directly which principle one should use when allocating one's donations (Figure 2.2). Should donations scale linearly with the number of beneficiaries (solid line) or rather sub-linearly so that one gives more per person to smaller groups of people (dashed line)? While the sub-linear function is consistent with scope neglect, participants preferred the linear function by a huge margin. This suggests that deep down most people don't actually believe that the value of saving an additional life diminishes as we save more lives. Scope neglect reflects our intuitive biases, not our considered judgments.

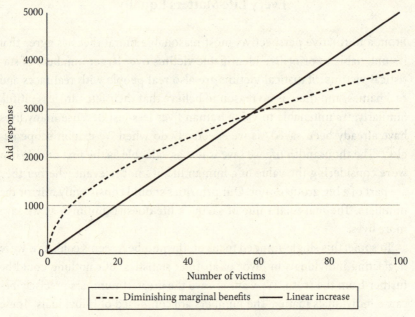

Figure 2.2 Aid Response as a Function of the Number of Victims

Note: Should your aid response scale linearly with the number of beneficiaries (solid line) or rather sub-linearly (dashed line), meaning that larger groups receive less per person? The latter is consistent with the idea that the marginal benefits of saving additional lives diminish as the number of saved lives increases. The former suggests that there are no such diminishing marginal benefits. The figure is a reproduction of Figure 1 and Figure 3 from (Dickert et al., 2015). Printed with permission from Elsevier.

Saving One Life Versus Saving the World

We can often increase our impact hugely by choosing the most effective ways of helping others. Scope neglect is one reason we frequently don't do that. Unfortunately, the result is often that we fail to avert substantial amounts of suffering that we could have averted. But that doesn't mean that scope neglect comes from a bad place. In fact, one could argue that the opposite is true.

There is a famous line in the *Talmud* (a central text in Judaism): "For anybody who preserves a single life it is counted as if he preserves an entire world" (*The Jerusalem Talmud*, 1999–2015, Sanhedrin 4:9). It very much expresses the spirit of scope neglect: Saving the whole world is no better than saving an individual life (Yudkowsky, 2007). But the way it expresses scope neglect is informative. The point is that if one person dies, that's already terrible, and if one person is saved, that's already fantastic. That suggests that the reason we suffer from scope neglect is not that we don't care about large numbers of deaths. Rather, it's because we already feel so strongly about an individual death. Our feelings may simply not get much stronger than that. Scope neglect is thus partly an unfortunate side effect of something good: that we feel so strongly for individuals who suffer.

We shouldn't let scope neglect affect us when we help others. If we have to make the choice, we should prioritize saving two lives over saving one life. We should definitely prioritize saving the world over saving a single individual. But we should appreciate that the sentiment the *Talmud* quote expresses comes from a good place: from powerful sympathy with the plight of our fellow humans. We want to retain that sympathy but adjust it slightly and channel it into helping them as effectively as we can.

Conclusion

There are huge differences in effectiveness between different ways of doing good. For instance, experts estimate that some global poverty charities are 100 times more effective than most other such charities. That means that donors have extraordinary opportunities to have an outsized impact. But by and large, they don't take them. We have seen that there are two main reasons.

First, most people vastly underestimate the differences in effectiveness between charities. They think that the differences in charity effectiveness are comparable to price differences for consumer goods, though they're actually much larger.

Second, people's help is driven by their feelings, and those feelings don't scale with the numbers. We already feel strongly about helping an individual victim and can't feel 100 times more about helping 100 victims. This means that teaching people about these large differences in effectiveness has a smaller effect on their behavior than one might have thought.

So, in two senses, we're neglecting the stakes: We don't know how large they are, and even when we do, our feelings can't quite grasp them. These are formidable obstacles to effective altruism.

References

Banerjee, A., Banerjee, A. V., & Duflo, E. (2011). *Poor economics: A radical rethinking of the way to fight global poverty*. PublicAffairs.

Baron, J., & Greene, J. (1996). Determinants of insensitivity to quantity in valuation of public goods: Contribution, warm glow, budget constraints, availability, and prominence. *Journal of Experimental Psychology: Applied, 2*(2), 107–125.

Berrett, J. L. (2020). *Burying the overhead myth and breaking the nonprofit starvation cycle: Identifying more valid measures and determinants of nonprofit efficiency* [Unpublished doctoral dissertation]. North Carolina State University.

Caviola, L., Schubert, S., Teperman, E., Moss, D., Greenberg, S., & Faber, N. S. (2020). Donors vastly underestimate differences in charities' effectiveness. *Judgment and Decision Making, 15*(4), 509–516.

Celizic, M. (2007, June 11). *"Baby Jessica" 20 years later*. Today. https://www.today.com/news/baby-jessica-20-years-later-2D80555271

Desvousges, W. H., Johnson, F. R., Dunford, R. W., Hudson, S. P., Wilson, K. N., & Boyle, K. J. (1993). Measuring natural resource damages with contingent valuation: Tests of validity and reliability. In J. A. Hausman (Ed.), *Contributions to economic analysis: Vol. 220. Contingent valuation: A critical assessment* (pp. 91–164). Elsevier.

Dickert, S., Västfjäll, D., Kleber, J., & Slovic, P. (2015). Scope insensitivity: The limits of intuitive valuation of human lives in public policy. *Journal of Applied Research in Memory and Cognition, 4*(3), 248–255.

Duda, R. (2023, June). *Global priorities research*. 80,000 Hours. Retrieved January 27, 2023, from https://80000hours.org/problem-profiles/global-priorities-research/

Duda, R. (2020, July). *Building effective altruism*. 80,000 Hours. Retrieved December 6, 2023, from https://80000hours.org/problem-profiles/promoting-effective-altruism/

Global Humanitarian Assistance. (2012). *Global humanitarian assistance report 2012*. https://devinit.org/wp-content/uploads/2012/07/GHA_Report_2012-Websingle.pdf

Guiding Eyes for the Blind. (n.d.). *Who we are*. Retrieved December 6, 2023, from https://www.guidingeyes.org/who-we-are/

Hart, P. S., Lane, D., & Chinn, S. (2018). The elusive power of the individual victim: Failure to find a difference in the effectiveness of charitable appeals focused on one compared to many victims. *PLOS ONE, 13*(7), Article e0199535.

Hollander, C. (2017, May 11). Update on our views on cataract surgery. *The GiveWell Blog*. Retrieved January 27, 2024 from https://blog.givewell.org/2017/05/11/update-on-our-views-on-cataract-surgery/

Hsee, C. K. (1996). The evaluability hypothesis: An explanation for preference reversals between joint and separate evaluations of alternatives. *Organizational Behavior and Human Decision Processes, 67*(3), 247–257.

Jamison, D. T., Breman, J. G., Measham, A. R., Alleyne, G., Claeson, M., Evans, D. B., Jha, P., Mills, A., & Musgrove, P. (2006). *Disease control priorities in developing countries*. World Bank Publications.

Jenni, K., & Loewenstein, G. (1997). Explaining the identifiable victim effect. *Journal of Risk and Uncertainty, 14*(3), 235–257.

Kahneman, D., & Knetsch, J. L. (1992). Valuing public goods: The purchase of moral satisfaction. *Journal of Environmental Economics and Management, 22*(1), 57–70.

Kogut, T., & Ritov, I. (2005a). The "identified victim" effect: An identified group, or just a single individual? *Journal of Behavioral Decision Making, 18*(3), 157–167.

Kogut, T., & Ritov, I. (2005b). The singularity effect of identified victims in separate and joint evaluations. *Organizational Behavior and Human Decision Processes, 97*(2), 106–116.

Maier, M., Wong, Y. C., & Feldman, G. (2023). Revisiting and rethinking the identifiable victim effect: Replication and extension of Small, Loewenstein, and Slovic (2007). *Collabra: Psychology, 9*(1). https://doi.org/10.1525/collabra.90203.

Majumder, R., Tai, Y. L., Ziano, I., & Feldman, G. (2022). Revisiting the impact of singularity on the identified victim effect: An unsuccessful replication and extension of Kogut and Ritov (2005) Study 2. https://osf.io/9qcpj/

Ord, T. (2013). *The moral imperative toward cost-effectiveness in global health*. Center for Global Development. https://cgdev.org/publication/moral-imperative-toward-cost-effectiveness-global-health

Parfit, D. (1978). Innumerate ethics. *Philosophy & Public Affairs, 7*(4), 285–301.

Quote Investigator. (2010). *A single death is a tragedy; a million deaths is a statistic*. Retrieved January 27, 2024, from https://quoteinvestigator.com/2010/05/21/death-statistic/

Slovic, P. (2007). "If I look at the mass I will never act": Psychic numbing and genocide. *Judgment and Decision Making, 2*(2), 79–95.

Slovic, P., Finucane, M. L., Peters, E., & MacGregor, D. G. (2007). The affect heuristic. *European Journal of Operational Research, 177*(3), 1333–1352.

Small, D. A., Loewenstein, G., & Slovic, P. (2007). Sympathy and callousness: The impact of deliberative thought on donations to identifiable and statistical victims. *Organizational Behavior and Human Decision Processes, 102*(2), 143–153.

The Jerusalem Talmud. (1999–2015). (H. W. Guggenheimer, Trans.). Sefaria/De Gruyter. https://www.sefaria.org/texts/Talmud/Yerushalmi

Todd, B. (2023, February). *The best solutions are far more effective than others*. 80,000 Hours. https://80000hours.org/articles/solutions/. Retrieved January 27, 2024.

Västfjäll, D., Slovic, P., Mayorga, M., & Peters, E. (2014). Compassion fade: Affect and charity are greatest for a single child in need. *PLOS ONE, 9*(6), Article e100115.

Yudkowsky, E. (2007, May 18). *One life against the world*. LessWrong. https://www.lesswrong.com/posts/xiHy3kFni8nsxfdcP/one-life-against-the-world

Zeckhauser, R., & Shepard, D. (1976). Where now for saving lives? *Law and Contemporary Problems, 40*(4), 5–45.

3
Distant Causes and Nearsighted Feelings

Most people prefer to help beneficiaries who are close to them. First, they tend to prioritize beneficiaries who are *spatially* close to them. They are *parochial*: They prioritize local or national charities over charities oriented toward distant countries. Second, they prefer to help beneficiaries who are *temporally* close to them. They are *presentist*: They prioritize presently existing people over people who will live in the future. And third, they are *speciesist*: They prioritize humans over other species. In other words, they favor helping beneficiaries who are biologically close to them. Thus, along three different axes of distance—spatial, temporal, and biological—most people prioritize beneficiaries who are close to them over more distant beneficiaries.

But as we will see in this chapter, it is often more effective to help more distant beneficiaries. Because most people don't prioritize distant beneficiaries, most opportunities to help them effectively haven't been taken. By contrast, there are fewer remaining opportunities to help people close to us effectively.

But why are we biased in favor of people close to us? The key cause is that our altruistic feelings are *nearsighted*. We evolved altruistic feelings for people we could ally ourselves with—and in the nature of things, those potential allies were close to us spatially, temporally, and biologically (Singer, 1981). Altruism toward distant strangers did not pay off, nor did altruism toward distant descendants or animals. By contrast, helping our local clan did pay off—it increased chances of survival and procreation—and our altruistic feelings evolved accordingly.

Parochialism

The most striking example of altruistic nearsightedness is parochialism: our tendency to prioritize people from our community, town, or country over people who are farther away from us. This tendency is epitomized by the oft-heard slogan "charity begins at home." Indeed, data suggests that only around one in ten US charitable dollars go to other countries, even though many international charities have proved to be highly effective, as we will see (Lilly

Family School of Philanthropy, 2023; Global Philanthropy Tracker, 2023). Why is that?

One part of the explanation is that people simply don't know how effective some charities helping people in distant countries are. In one of our studies, we presented American participants with a charity that was said to help sick people in India and another charity that was said to help sick people in their local community (Caviola et al., 2020). (They were said to be similar in other regards.) We found that even though it is, in fact, typically much more effective to help people in developing countries—primarily due to them having more dire needs—participants thought that the two charities had about the same level of cost-effectiveness. In line with that, most people preferred giving to the charity supporting sick people in their local community.

However, participants who were informed that the charity helping sick people in India is more effective were more disposed to give to that charity than participants who weren't provided such information. This indicates that one reason that people prioritize giving to domestic charities is that they don't know that it would be more effective to give to the global poor. Some may doubt that money sent overseas will reach the intended beneficiaries (Knowles & Sullivan, 2017).

But erroneous beliefs are only part of why people tend to prioritize domestic charities over charities helping people in developing countries. Even many participants who were informed that the charity helping sick people in India is more effective chose to support the charity helping sick people in their local community. This suggests that another reason that people donate to local or domestic causes is that they simply have a preference for them. As we saw in Chapter 1, people have many preferences that compete with their desire to give effectively. The preference for local or domestic causes is another such preference, in addition to people's preference for mitigating emergencies and their preference for causes they have a personal connection with (Baron & Szymanska, 2011).

But people don't just have these preferences for local and domestic causes; they also think it is right to have them. Prioritizing people close to us is the norm, just as it is the norm to use our feelings when we decide how to help. People who support distant people over people close to them can be negatively judged (Everett et al., 2018; Law et al., 2022; Chapter 1). These parochial norms reinforce people's behavior and make it more difficult to change. (But they need not necessarily make it impossible—an issue we return to in Chapter 8, where we look at norm change as a strategy for spreading effective altruism.)

To explain where parochialism comes from, it is natural to take an evolutionary perspective. As Peter Singer explained in his classic book *The Expanding Circle* (1981), our altruistic feelings evolved to facilitate collaboration among small groups of people (Bowles, 2008; Choi & Bowles, 2007; Rusch, 2014). In the ancestral environment, people lived in small bands or clans, which often were on hostile terms with other groups. That meant that being altruistic to out-groups was not necessarily conducive to survival and procreation. As a result, our disposition to help our in-group evolved to be much stronger than our disposition to help out-groups. Our "circle of moral concern," to use Singer's words, was drawn very narrowly.

Besides erroneous beliefs and pure parochialism, there are also other causes that lead people to prioritize beneficiaries who are close to them. Physical distance often correlates with various factors that make people more inclined to give support (Law et al., 2022; Nagel & Waldmann, 2013). Local problems tend to be more salient and appear more often in the news. Due to availability bias—our tendency to focus on issues at the forefront of our minds—we are more likely to support salient causes (Schwarz & Vaughn, 2002). Similarly, we are usually more likely to have a personal connection with local problems. Thus, several mechanisms likely contribute to our tendency to neglect distant beneficiaries.

Can parochialism be addressed? Our moral circle is certainly not set in stone: As Singer (1981) shows, it has expanded with time. In many parts of the world, racism and other forms of discrimination in favor of the in-group used to be stronger than they are today. Thus, parochialism has arguably declined over the past centuries. Still, we are far from fully impartial, as evidenced by the fact that many people think they should prioritize people in their own countries and communities over people in distant countries.

But some have another attitude, such as people in the effective altruism community. In *The Expanding Circle*, Peter Singer (1981) didn't just argue for the *descriptive* thesis that our circle of moral concern has, in fact, expanded with time. He also argued for the *normative* thesis that we should keep expanding it. This view has been adopted by the effective altruism community. Thus, effective altruists argue that we should fully reject parochialism and endorse moral impartiality.

In line with this, many effective altruists focus on helping people in some of the world's poorest countries. In fact, two of the best-known effective altruist organizations, GiveWell and Giving What We Can, are primarily associated with global poverty and health. After its inception in 2007, GiveWell soon concluded that the best global poverty charities are more effective than domestic charities targeting Americans. "Your dollar goes further overseas": The poorest people in the world often lack access to basic health care, and consequently, even small donations covering these needs can have a remarkable impact (GiveWell, n.d.). Similar reasoning led the giving community Giving What We Can to focus on global poverty and health when it was set up in 2009 (though Giving What We Can has subsequently opened up to other causes; Hutchinson, 2016; Singer, 2015). We will discuss effective altruist work on global poverty and health in more detail in Chapter 9.

Whereas effective altruists reject parochialism, most people find it more intuitive to prioritize nearby beneficiaries. However, some evidence suggests that if people reflect on these issues more carefully, they become more morally impartial. Philosophers have devised a thought experiment called "the veil of ignorance" to test different moral decisions and ethical theories (Harsanyi, 1955; Rawls, 1971). The idea is that when we consider what to do from a moral point of view, we should imagine that we don't know any of our characteristics: where we live, what gender and ethnicity we have, how wealthy we are, and so on. Such ignorance will make us more unbiased and lead to more morally correct decisions, the reasoning goes.

How would people prioritize between charities that help distant poor people and charities that help their compatriots from behind the veil of ignorance? In a study, Karen Huang, Joshua Greene, and Max Bazerman (2019) investigated that question. Specifically, they asked American participants whether they would prioritize an effective charity helping Indian beneficiaries over a less effective charity helping American beneficiaries. They found that participants were significantly more likely to prioritize the charity supporting Indian beneficiaries when they imagined themselves to be behind the veil of ignorance than when they did not. This gives some support to the notion that people's intuitive parochialism may not be as firm as one might have thought. We explore how philosophical arguments can affect people's moral values in more detail in Chapter 8.

Presentism

Just as most people prioritize spatially close beneficiaries, they also prioritize temporally close beneficiaries. Most people are presentists: They prefer helping currently existing beneficiaries over beneficiaries who will live in the future. In line with that, we're making relatively small long-term investments as a society. For instance, we are doing less to mitigate climate change than we likely would have done if we were more concerned with the welfare of future people.

A study by Lucius Caviola, Amanda Geiser, and Joshua Lewis provides experimental evidence of presentism (Geiser et al., 2022). They presented participants with two charities: one charity focused on the present (on causes like global poverty and health) and another charity focused on the future (on causes like prevention of pandemics, climate change, and nuclear war). They asked the participants which of the two charities they would donate $100 to and found that nearly two-thirds (65.5%) chose the charity focusing on present causes, while only the remaining third (34.5%) chose the charity focusing on future causes.

Several factors contribute to this tendency to prioritize causes relating to the present. Most people tend to prioritize the present over the future even when it comes to their own consumption. We are impatient: We would rather have a smaller sum today than a slightly larger sum in the future (even adjusting for inflation and related issues). In the words of economists, we have a relatively high *temporal discount rate*: We discount the value of the future relative to the present (Doyle, 2013; Frederick et al., 2002; Greaves, 2017a; van den Bos & McClure, 2013). As economists have demonstrated, this leads us to save too little for retirement and to many other suboptimal outcomes in our personal lives (Fehr, 2002). But most of us also have a high *social* temporal discount rate—a high temporal discount rate when it comes to social and political issues. Many want the government to spend more today instead of saving for the future. Similarly, many voters don't want us to cut greenhouse gas emissions for the sake of the future, instead prioritizing present consumption. This is a major reason we don't do more to combat climate change (Jacquet et al., 2013).

Over longer time periods, these dynamics are likely exacerbated by the fact that people who forgo present consumption for the sake of the future won't be able to enjoy that future. Instead, it will benefit future generations. And people may not want to forgo consumption today for the sake of a tomorrow that they will never see. Relatedly, since future people by definition don't exist yet, they cannot advocate for themselves. In this regard, they differ from many groups that are discriminated against here and now. That may partially explain why less has been done to benefit potential future people.

Just like parochialism, presentism can be explained from an evolutionary perspective. In the ancestral environment, people could only influence the near-term future, meaning there was little point in trying to help distant descendants. Moreover, future people weren't useful as allies—since they could not reciprocate help—which further reduced the incentives to help them. Hence, we evolved to be temporally partial, just as we evolved to be spatially partial.

It's possible, however, that presentism doesn't run quite as deep as one might think and that it (just like parochialism) can be reduced by changing the framing. In the study on donations to causes relating to the present and the future, Caviola and his colleagues tested whether a perspective-taking exercise could change people's donation choices (Geiser et al., 2022). Participants were told to take the perspective of a person living 200 years from now and were subsequently asked to indicate how this future person would want currently living people to donate. It turned out that participants who had engaged in this perspective-taking exercise were significantly more likely to prioritize the cause relating to the future in an ensuing donation task compared with the control group (47.5% vs. 34.5%). However, this is just one study, and we need more research on the effects of philosophical arguments on people's moral views on the long-term future (Chapter 8).

Temporal partiality is undoubtedly an important reason that the long-term future is so neglected, but it is not the only reason. Another reason is likely that temporally distant problems are less salient than temporally close problems, just as spatially distant problems are less salient than spatially close problems. In fact, temporally distant problems are probably even less salient than spatially distant problems. Spatial distance can, to an extent, be bridged by modern technology. While problems in distant countries were decidedly lacking in salience before the advent of the telegraph, the radio, TV, and the internet, they are much more salient today, thanks to real-time reporting. This may contribute to greater concern for suffering people in distant countries. But temporal distance cannot be similarly bridged. We cannot provide live reports of the distant future the way we can provide live reports of events in distant countries. As a result, the distant future is still very much lacking in salience. This lack of salience may be an important reason that future people are so neglected.

We investigated how the fact that the long-term future isn't salient affects people's judgments of the moral badness of human extinction in a study with Nadira Faber (Schubert et al., 2019). In the philosopher Derek Parfit's famous book *Reasons and Persons* (1984) there is a thought experiment intended to illustrate the unique moral badness of human extinction, as well as potential biases that affect our judgments of that badness. Parfit asked us to consider three outcomes:

a. Peace
b. A nuclear war killing 99% of all currently living people
c. A nuclear war killing everyone

The first outcome is obviously the best, and the last outcome is obviously the worst, from a moral point of view. The more interesting question is what difference is greater: that between (a) and (b) or that between (b) and (c)?

Parfit predicted that most people would say that the difference between (a) and (b) is greater. That is because they would look at the number of deaths, and in such terms, the difference between (a) and (b) is indeed greater. But Parfit himself thought that the difference between (b) and (c) is greater because only human extinction would lead to a permanent loss of the future. We could recover from a catastrophe killing 99% of the global population, but we couldn't recover from human extinction. That's what makes it uniquely bad, in Parfit's view.

Together with Nadira Faber, we devised a series of experiments intended to test Parfit's hypothesis that most people would find the difference between (a) and (b) greater (Schubert et al., 2019). Using a slightly modified setup (where, e.g., 80% rather than 99% were said to die in scenario (b)), we found support for Parfit's hypothesis. In two online studies, around 80% of participants thought the difference (in terms of badness) between no one dying and nearly everyone dying was greater than the difference between nearly everyone dying and everyone dying.

But we also found that this is partly because the long-term effects of extinction aren't salient to people. In another condition, we told participants to "remember to consider the long-term consequences of the three outcomes." In this condition, significantly greater shares of the participants in the two studies (50% and 39%, respectively) thought that the difference between nearly everyone dying and everyone dying was the larger one. In other words, simply making the long-term consequences of the outcomes salient led more people to choose the option that implies that human extinction is uniquely bad. This speaks to the important role of salience. People tend to neglect long-term effects, focusing on more salient near-term consequences.

This can make them undervalue interventions with substantial long-term effects, such as prevention of an existential catastrophe (human extinction or permanent civilizational collapse; Bostrom, 2002, 2013).

Many researchers think that the risk of an existential catastrophe is substantial. For instance, the philosopher Toby Ord (2020) argues that there is a 1 in 6 chance of an existential catastrophe in the 21st century, the greatest risks stemming, in his judgment, from emerging technologies such as advanced artificial intelligence and synthetically manufactured viruses. Moreover, Ord and many other researchers agree with Parfit that it would be a moral disaster if human civilization collapsed or perished altogether since it would mean that a potentially great future never came to exist. In line with that, preventing an existential catastrophe is one of the most popular strategies to affect the long-term future within the effective altruism community.

But there are some arguments against Parfit's view that human extinction would be uniquely bad. One of them is that the future simply might turn out to be so bad that it would be better if it never came into existence. A related argument is that we should put special moral weight on suffering, meaning that even if the future would be good in some ways, it might not be worth the price in terms of additional suffering (Benatar, 2006; Gloor, 2019; Knutsson, 2021; Smart, 1958; Tomasik, 2017). A third argument is based on the so-called *person-affecting view*, which says that an act can only be good if it helps specific people. Bringing new people into existence is morally neutral, according to the person-affecting view—and if so, human extinction isn't as bad as Parfit and many effective altruists think (Broome, 2004; Greaves, 2017b; Narveson, 1973; Rabinowicz, 2009). It would still be bad since it would cut many people's lives short, but it wouldn't be qualitatively worse than a non-extinction catastrophe. The fact that human extinction would cause many potential future people never to be born wouldn't make it a uniquely bad outcome.

Do laypeople agree with the person-affecting view, and if so, might that be a reason that we don't invest more in preventing human extinction? Lucius Caviola has studied that issue with David Althaus, Andreas Mogensen, and Geoffrey Goodwin (Caviola, Althaus, et al., 2022). They asked participants whether adding new happy people to the world would make it a morally better place. On average, participants thought that it did. In other words, most people don't seem to hold person-affecting intuitions. These results suggest that the person-affecting view may not be a key reason we don't invest more in preventing human extinction.

Besides people's moral views and the fact that the long-term future isn't salient, another potential reason that people prioritize the present is that they think that we cannot meaningfully address the long-term future. One argument is that the effects of anything we do will simply "wash out" over longer time frames: that even if an action has positive consequences in the short run, it is impossible to know what the long-run consequences will be (Webb, 2021). Philosophers call such worries "cluelessness": that we are "clueless" about the long-term effects of our actions (Greaves, 2016; Lenman, 2000). If we are indeed clueless, it may appear hopeless to try to help people who will live in the future.

These worries should be taken seriously since long-run predictions are indeed very difficult (Tarsney, 2023). However, there are some actions whose consequences may be more foreseeable. If there's an existential catastrophe, then by definition humanity's future potential will not be realized. That means that if it's possible to reduce the likelihood of an existential catastrophe, it may be possible to affect the long-term future positively. This argument is another reason that many effective altruists focus on reducing existential risk, besides the aforementioned belief that the level of existential risk in the near term is high. Existential risk mitigation may be less affected by cluelessness concerns than other attempts to affect the long-term future.

In recent years, an increasing number of effective altruists have come to believe that making the long-term future go well is the highest-impact cause. These *longtermists* acknowledge that it is hard to affect the long-term future positively but believe that it is not impossible. Both the longtermist philosophy and potential strategies to affect the long-term future are introduced at length in William MacAskill's recent *What We Owe the Future* (2022), but we will also discuss it in brief in Chapter 9.

Speciesism

So far, we have seen that people are inclined to neglect spatially and temporally distant beneficiaries. But they also neglect biologically distant beneficiaries: non-human animals. In the philosopher Peter Singer's words, most people are speciesist; that is, they exhibit "a prejudice or attitude of bias in favor of the interests of members of [their] own species and against those of members of other species" (1975/2002, p. 6). Each year, more than 70 billion land animals (as well as fish and shellfish) are killed for human consumption (Sanders, 2018). Many of them live under very poor conditions on factory farms. Yet even though charity evaluators estimate that it is remarkably cheap to help them, only a tiny fraction of charitable donations are directed toward animal welfare. In fact, only 3% of US charitable donations are allocated to organizations supporting animals and the environment combined (Anderson, 2018).

Why is that? Why do people prioritize humans over animals? One hypothesis is that it's because humans are more intelligent or have some other potentially relevant mental capacity. According to this hypothesis, people prioritize humans over animals because they believe (a) that certain mental capacities are morally relevant and (b) that humans have those capacities but animals lack them.

Together with Guy Kahane and Nadira Faber, we studied this question in a series of experiments. We presented participants with hypothetical scenarios where they had to choose between saving more or less mentally advanced animals of the same species. We found that the participants consistently prioritized the more mentally advanced animals, providing support for the view that people consider mental capacities morally relevant and that this could be part of the reason they prioritize humans over animals (Caviola, Schubert, et al., 2022).

Interestingly, the perceived connection between mental capacities and moral value may also go in the reverse direction. In other words, people may lower animals' perceived mental capacities because they think that animals are less morally valuable. Brock Bastian and his colleagues have shown that when meat-eaters are reminded that eating meat causes animals to suffer, they tend to deny that animals have minds (Bastian et al., 2012). This suggests that they engage in motivated reasoning: They perceive animals' mental capacities to be weaker than they are because they don't want to change their views of animals' moral value.

But while beliefs about the mental capacities of animals—whether grounded in motivated reasoning or not—are part of why people prioritize humans over animals, it is easy to see that they cannot be the full explanation. There are humans (e.g., infants and severely cognitively impaired people) whose mental capacities are no more advanced than those of animals, and yet people tend to think that they are more morally valuable than animals. This seems obvious from everyday experience, but we also verified it experimentally. In moral dilemmas pitting humans against animals, we found that most people prioritized saving the humans even when the animals in question were said to have the same or, notably, greater mental capacities (Caviola, Schubert, et al., 2022). This suggests that most people prioritize humans over animals in part purely because they are members of the human species. The current evidence thus suggests that most people are indeed speciesist—they discriminate based on species membership alone. (Though we didn't test the effect of mere differences in appearance between humans and animals, which would be worth studying in future research; Timmerman, 2018).

Philosophers have long argued that speciesism is at the root of people's tendency to prioritize humans over animals (Horta, 2010; Singer, 1975/2002). In a 2019 paper, Lucius Caviola, Jim Everett, and Nadira Faber validated this hypothesis empirically and defined speciesism psychologically. They showed that speciesism is a temporally stable psychological construct with clear interpersonal differences and that it predicts a range of behaviors, including food and donation choices. They also found that speciesism correlates with other forms of prejudice, such as racism, sexism, and homophobia. In line with these findings, Kristof Dhont and his colleagues (2014) have found that discrimination against animals correlates with social dominance orientation, a broad moral orientation whose core is a favorable attitude toward existing social hierarchies.

But what does it mean, more precisely, to discriminate against individuals based on their species membership? In our research, we've discovered two forms of speciesism, which are quite different (Caviola, Schubert, et al., 2022). First, many people believe that individuals of any species should prioritize members of their own species: a view we call *species-relativism*. According to this view, dogs should be partial in favor of dogs and pigs should be partial in favor of pigs, just as humans should be partial in favor of humans. Species-relativism is in some ways analogous to our tendency to prioritize our family members over strangers. Typically, we prioritize our family members not because we consider them intrinsically more morally valuable but because we think we stand in a special relationship with them, generating special obligations (Jeske, 2019). Moreover, we think that other people are justified in prioritizing their family over strangers (and indeed judge them if they don't; McManus et al., 2020). Similarly, species-relativists think that members of a species have special obligations toward other members of their species and should prioritize them. Because humans are the dominant species on Earth, this approach happens to favor human interests. But if another species had been dominant, they would have been similarly justified in putting their interests first, according to species-relativism.

A skeptic might wonder whether species-relativists would stick to this view if another species came to rule the world. And the notion that mere species membership creates special obligations to fellow species members can certainly be criticized from a philosophical point of view. But regardless of that, species-relativism is not the whole story. We also found evidence for another form of speciesism, which we call *species-absolutism*: the view that all beings (both humans and animals) should prioritize humans over animals, simply because they are humans. According to this view, humans are more valuable than animals in an absolute sense, independently of their relative mental capacities and the relationship between decision maker and beneficiaries. Thus, species-absolutism doesn't seem to be grounded in any empirical differences between humans and animals. It's therefore difficult to see that it could be given a philosophical justification.

Speciesism is deeply ingrained in contemporary society. Large-scale exploitation of animals plays a central role in the economy, and that plausibly reinforces speciesist attitudes. We continue to eat animals on a massive scale, which means that we have a strong incentive to devalue animals. Stopping the consumption of animals would require us to change our way of life, and some of us would suffer substantial economic consequences. Therefore, we are motivated to retain speciesist beliefs (Bastian et al., 2012).

Relatedly, speciesism is likely in part culturally acquired. In a series of experiments, Lucius Caviola and his colleagues Matti Wilks, Guy Kahane, and Paul Bloom found that children between the ages of 6 and 9 are much less likely to prioritize humans over animals than adults are (Wilks et al., 2021). For example, children find a dog's life almost as valuable as a human life; and they also find pigs more valuable than adults do. This suggests that at least some components of speciesism may emerge late in development, possibly during adolescence. It may be that children or teenagers at some point assimilate the moral views that prop up our current treatment of animals (i.e., speciesism).

But even though speciesism is likely in part culturally acquired, it's also plausible that it is partly innate. Just as we didn't evolve to be altruistic toward spatially and temporally distant people, we arguably didn't evolve to be altruistic toward animals. In the ancestral environment, humans could use animals for food and other purposes. Thus, extensive altruism toward animals was usually not adaptive, and therefore didn't evolve.

So far, we have focused on discrimination of animals in favor of humans: what we can call *anthropocentric speciesism*. No doubt, this is the most important manifestation of speciesism. But it's not the only one. Already in his classical book *Animal Liberation*, Peter Singer (1975/2002) suggested that people also discriminate against some types of non-human animals in favor of others. Caviola and his colleagues' research (2019) has confirmed that that is indeed the case. For instance, as we saw in Chapter 1, people tend to prioritize pets (e.g., dogs) over other animals (e.g., pigs): what we might call *pet speciesism*. People give much more to pet sanctuaries than to charities that improve conditions at factory farms, even though the latter are likely more effective (Animal Charity Evaluators, 2024).

While anthropocentric speciesism and pet speciesism are related, they are also psychologically different in some interesting ways. In a study, Lucius Caviola and Valerio Capraro (2020) found that when people are prompted to think more deliberately and less emotionally, pet speciesism grew weaker, whereas anthropocentric speciesism grew stronger. People tend to prioritize dogs over pigs because they feel more strongly for dogs on a gut level but become more even-handed when prompted to reflect. By contrast, further reflection strengthened people's tendency to prioritize humans over animals. This indicates that the belief that humans are more valuable than animals is not just a fleeting emotional reaction. Instead, it is a view many people endorse deep down.

Effective altruists reject speciesism, and many find promoting animal welfare a worthwhile cause (Thomas, 2023). In particular, many effective altruists believe that improving the conditions for animals at factory farms can be highly effective. Exactly how impactful it is depends on many complex moral and empirical considerations, such as what experiences of pleasure and pain different animal species have (Birch, 2022; Birch et al., 2020; Fischer, 2022; Muehlhauser, 2018). These questions are extremely difficult, and there can no doubt be reasonable disagreement on them (see Chapter 5). We will look closer at effective altruist work on promoting animal welfare in Chapter 9.

Conclusion

When we're looking to do good, it's important to consider helping beneficiaries that are spatially, temporally, and biologically far away from us. Interventions aimed at helping these distant beneficiaries are often particularly effective. For instance, some of the most effective charities help the global poor. Likewise, work aimed to benefit future people (e.g., by reducing the risk of an existential disaster) can have a very high impact. And it can be very effective to help animals (e.g., by addressing the dismal conditions at factory farms).

And yet only a small fraction of altruistic efforts is targeted toward these effective distant causes. Instead, most people support beneficiaries who are close to them, even though that means that their help will typically be much less effective than it could be. We neglect distant beneficiaries because our altruistic feelings are nearsighted. We are intuitively parochial, presentist, and speciesist. These obstacles are a major cause of why our help is often less effective than it could be.

References

Anderson, J. (2018). *Giving to animals: New data on who and how*. Faunalytics. Retrieved January 29, 2024 from https://faunalytics.org/giving-to-animals-new-data-who-how/#

Animal Charity Evaluators. (2024, January). *Why farmed animals?* Retrieved January 27, 2024 from https://animalcharityevaluators.org/donation-advice/why-farmed-animals/.

Baron, J., & Szymanska, E. (2011). Heuristics and biases in charity. In D. M. Oppenheimer & C. Y. Olivola (Eds.), *The science of giving: Experimental approaches to the study of charity* (pp. 215–235). Psychology Press.

Bastian, B., Loughnan, S., Haslam, N., & Radke, H. R. M. (2012). Don't mind meat? The denial of mind to animals used for human consumption. *Personality & Social Psychology Bulletin, 38*(2), 247–256.

Benatar, D. (2006). *Better never to have been: The harm of coming into existence*. Oxford University Press.

Birch, J. (2022). The search for invertebrate consciousness. *Nous, 56*(1), 133–153.

Birch, J., Schnell, A. K., & Clayton, N. S. (2020). Dimensions of animal consciousness. *Trends in Cognitive Sciences, 24*(10), 789–801.

Bostrom, N. (2002). Existential risks: Analyzing human extinction scenarios and related hazards. *Journal of Evolution and Technology, 9*(1), 1–30.

Bostrom, N. (2013). Existential risk prevention as global priority. *Global Policy, 4*(1), 15–31.

Bowles, S. (2008). Being human: Conflict: Altruism's midwife. *Nature, 456*(7220), 326–327.

Broome, J. (2004). *Weighing lives*. Oxford University Press.

Caviola, L., Althaus, D., Mogensen, A. L., & Goodwin, G. P. (2022). Population ethical intuitions. *Cognition, 218*, Article 104941.

Caviola, L., & Capraro, V. (2020). Liking but devaluing animals: Emotional and deliberative paths to speciesism. *Social Psychological and Personality Science, 11*(8), 1080–1088.

Caviola, L., Everett, J. A. C., & Faber, N. S. (2019). The moral standing of animals: Towards a psychology of speciesism. *Journal of Personality and Social Psychology, 116*(6), 1011–1029.

Caviola, L., Schubert, S., Kahane, G., & Faber, N. S. (2022). Humans first: Why people value animals less than humans. *Cognition, 225,* Article 105139.

Caviola, L., Schubert, S., & Nemirow, J. (2020). The many obstacles to effective giving. *Judgment and Decision Making, 15*(2), 159–172.

Choi, J.-K., & Bowles, S. (2007). The coevolution of parochial altruism and war. *Science, 318*(5850), 636–640.

Dhont, K., Hodson, G., Costello, K., & MacInnis, C. C. (2014). Social dominance orientation connects prejudicial human–human and human–animal relations. *Personality and Individual Differences, 61–62,* 105–108.

Doyle, J. R. (2013). Survey of time preference, delay discounting models. *Judgment and Decision Making, 8*(2), 116–135.

Everett, J. A. C., Faber, N. S., Savulescu, J., & Crockett, M. J. (2018). The costs of being consequentialist: Social inference from instrumental harm and impartial beneficence. *Journal of Experimental Social Psychology, 79,* 200–216.

Fehr, E. (2002). The economics of impatience. *Nature, 415*(6869), 269–272.

Fischer, B. (2022, October 31). *An introduction to the Moral Weight Project.* Rethink Priorities. Retrieved January 27, 2024 from https://rethinkpriorities.org/publications/an-introduction-to-the-moral-weight-project

Frederick, S., Loewenstein, G., & O'Donoghue, T. (2002). Time discounting and time preference: A critical review. *Journal of Economic Literature, 40*(2), 351–401.

Geiser, A., Caviola, L., & Lewis, J. (2022). *Perspective-taking and helping distant others* [Unpublished manuscript]. Department of Psychology, Harvard University.

GiveWell. (n.d.). *Your dollar goes further overseas.* Retrieved February 10, 2023, from https://www.givewell.org/giving101/Your-dollar-goes-further-overseas

Global Philanthropy Tracker (2023). Lilly Family School of Philanthropy. https://scholarworks.iupui.edu/server/api/core/bitstreams/09eba67a-185b-4f3c-ab40-3869ee430079/content

Gloor, L. (2019, August). *The case for suffering-focused ethics.* Center on Long-Term Risk. Retrieved January 27, 2024 from https://longtermrisk.org/the-case-for-suffering-focused-ethics/

Greaves, H. (2016). Cluelessness. *Proceedings of the Aristotelian Society, 116*(3), 311–339.

Greaves, H. (2017a). Discounting for public policy: A survey. *Economics & Philosophy, 33*(3), 391–439.

Greaves, H. (2017b). Population axiology. *Philosophy Compass, 12*(11), Article e12442.

Harsanyi, J. C. (1955). Cardinal welfare, individualistic ethics, and interpersonal comparisons of utility. *The Journal of Political Economy, 63*(4), 309–321.

Horta, O. (2010). What is speciesism? *Journal of Agricultural & Environmental Ethics, 23*(3), 243–266.

Huang, K., Greene, J. D., & Bazerman, M. (2019). Veil-of-ignorance reasoning favors the greater good. *Proceedings of the National Academy of Sciences of the United States of America, 116*(48), 23989–23995.

Hutchinson, M. (2016, April 22). *Giving what we can is cause neutral.* Effective Altruism Forum. https://forum.effectivealtruism.org/posts/tLdtftZakmpWq73kA/giving-what-we-can-is-cause-neutral

Jacquet, J., Hagel, K., Hauert, C., Marotzke, J., Röhl, T., & Milinski, M. (2013). Intra- and intergenerational discounting in the climate game. *Nature Climate Change, 3*(12), 1025–1028.

Jeske, D. (2019, August 6). Special obligations. In E. N. Zalta (Ed.), *Stanford encyclopedia of philosophy* (winter 2021 ed.). https://plato.stanford.edu/archives/win2021/entries/special-obligations/

Knowles, S., & Sullivan, T. (2017). Does charity begin at home or overseas? *Nonprofit and Voluntary Sector Quarterly, 46*(5), 944–962.

Knutsson, S. (2021). The world destruction argument. *Inquiry, 64*(10), 1004–1023.

Law, K. F., Campbell, D., & Gaesser, B. (2022). Biased benevolence: The perceived morality of effective altruism across social distance. *Personality & Social Psychology Bulletin, 48*(3), 426–444.

Lenman, J. (2000). Consequentialism and cluelessness. *Philosophy & Public Affairs, 29*(4), 342–370.

Lilly Family School of Philanthropy. (2023, June 20). *Giving USA: Total U.S. charitable giving declined in 2022 to $499.33 billion following two years of record generosity.* https://philanthropy.iupui.edu/news-events/news/_news/2023/giving-usa-total-us-charitable-giving-declined-in-2022-to-49933-billion-following-two-years-of-record-generosity.html

MacAskill, W. (2022). *What we owe the future: A million-year view.* Oneworld Publications.

McManus, R. M., Kleiman-Weiner, M., & Young, L. (2020). What we owe to family: The impact of special obligations on moral judgment. *Psychological Science, 31*(3), 227–242.

Muehlhauser, L. (2018, January). *2017 report on consciousness and moral patienthood.* Open Philanthropy. https://www.openphilanthropy.org/research/2017-report-on-consciousness-and-moral-patienthood/

Nagel, J., & Waldmann, M. R. (2013). Deconfounding distance effects in judgments of moral obligation. *Journal of Experimental Psychology. Learning, Memory, and Cognition, 39*(1), 237–252.

Narveson, J. (1973). Moral problems of population. *The Monist, 57*(1), 62–86.

Ord, T. (2020). *The precipice: Existential risk and the future of humanity.* Hachette Books.

Parfit, D. (1984). *Reasons and persons.* Oxford University Press.

Rabinowicz, W. (2009). Broome and the intuition of neutrality. *Philosophical Issues, 19,* 389–411.

Rawls, J. (1971). *A theory of justice.* Belknap Press.

Rusch, H. (2014). The evolutionary interplay of intergroup conflict and altruism in humans: A review of parochial altruism theory and prospects for its extension. *Proceedings of the Royal Society B: Biological Sciences, 281*(1794), Article 20141539.

Sanders, B. (2018, October 10). *Global animal slaughter statistics and charts.* Faunalytics. Retrieved January 27, 2024 from https://faunalytics.org/global-animal-slaughter-statistics-and-charts/

Schubert, S., Caviola, L., & Faber, N. S. (2019). The psychology of existential risk: Moral judgments about human extinction. *Scientific Reports, 9*(1), Article 15100.

Schwarz, N., & Vaughn, L. A. (2002). The availability heuristic revisited: Ease of recall and content of recall as distinct sources of information. In D. Kahneman, T. Gilovich, & D. Griffin (Eds.), *Heuristics and biases: The psychology of intuitive judgment* (pp. 103–119). Cambridge University Press.

Singer, P. (1975/2002). *Animal liberation.* Ecco, Harper Collins Publishers.

Singer, P. (1981). *The expanding circle: Ethics and sociobiology.* Clarendon Press.

Singer, P. (2015). *The most good you can do: How effective altruism is changing ideas about living ethically.* Yale University Press.

Smart, R. N. (1958). Negative utilitarianism. *Mind, 67*(268), 542–543.

Tarsney, C. (2023). The epistemic challenge to longtermism. *Synthese, 201,* Article 195. https://doi.org/10.1007/s11229-023-04153-y

Thomas, J. (2023). *The farm animal movement: Effective altruism, venture philanthropy, and the fight to end factory farming in America.* Lantern Publishing & Media.

Timmerman, T. (2018). You're probably not really a speciesist. *Pacific Philosophical Quarterly, 99*(4), 683–701.

Tomasik, B. (2017, December 23). *Are happiness and suffering symmetric?* Reducing Suffering. Retrieved January 27, 2024 from https://reducing-suffering.org/happiness-suffering-symmetric/

van den Bos, W., & McClure, S. M. (2013). Towards a general model of temporal discounting. *Journal of the Experimental Analysis of Behavior, 99*(1), 58–73.

Webb, D. (2021, March 25). *Formalising the "washing out hypothesis."* Effective Altruism Forum. https://forum.effectivealtruism.org/posts/z2DkdXgPitqf98AvY/formalising-the-washing-out-hypothesis

Wilks, M., Caviola, L., Kahane, G., & Bloom, P. (2021). Children prioritize humans over animals less than adults do. *Psychological Science, 32*(1), 27–38.

4
Tough Prioritizing

To help effectively, you need to support the most effective causes. As we've seen, people don't always do that. They choose how to help based on their feelings, and they don't necessarily feel strongly about the most effective causes. They may lack a personal connection with them or feel that the beneficiaries are too distant.

But you also need to do something else to help effectively. It's not enough to support the most effective causes. You also have to choose not to support other, less effective causes.

If we give resources to less effective causes, we will have fewer resources to give to the most effective causes. Every dollar that goes to a less effective charity is a dollar that could have gone to one of the most effective charities—a dollar that could have had a much greater impact. And every hour we spend on a less effective project is an hour that we could have spent more effectively.

So, helping effectively is not just about what we do. It is also about what we don't do. More often than not, it means abstaining from supporting some causes that we feel deserve our support. Prioritizing some charities entails deprioritizing others, and deprioritization is one of the toughest aspects of helping effectively.

People are often positive about effectiveness in the abstract. As we saw in Chapter 1, many people say that effectiveness is one of their key criteria when choosing a charity. But when they say that, they are likely not thinking about all its implications. In particular, they are likely not considering the fact that it can imply not giving to some charities that they feel strongly about. Many are decidedly less enthusiastic about that. People don't like to deprioritize charities that they feel are worthy of their help. And yet there is no other choice. If we want to prioritize the most effective charities, we have to deprioritize less effective charities. They are two sides of the same coin.

In some cases, it is more salient that we have to make tough deprioritization decisions to be effective. William MacAskill (2015, pp. 34–35) offers an example from the civil war in Rwanda in the 1990s. There were so many injured people that the healthcare system became overwhelmed. Some of the patients were badly injured, and there was only a small chance that they could be saved. Under normal circumstances, they would of course have been treated; but in this difficult triage situation, patients with a decent chance of survival had to be prioritized. Of course, most people feel bad about that; but since a war makes it so salient that such deprioritization decisions are necessary to save more people, they may still be inclined to accept it (Caviola et al., 2021; McKie & Richardson, 2011).

But the psychology of emergencies differs from the psychology of non-emergencies. The way we think about war triage or drowning children is not the same as the way we think about charitable donations (Chapter 1). Emergencies are more urgent, and therefore it feels more pressing—or even obligatory—to choose the most effective option. People are more inclined to be effective when they help wounded soldiers or drowning children than when they choose between different charities in the comfort of their homes.

In an emergency, most people accept that we must prioritize some and deprioritize others to be effective. But when it comes to charity, they often find it less important to do so. When given the option, they often split their donations between two charities. In a study we conducted with Jason Nemirow, we asked participants how they would allocate $100 across two charities, one of which was said to be highly effective and one of which was said to be of average effectiveness (Caviola, Schubert, & Nemirow, 2020). Since the most effective charities consistently do more good per dollar, you would maximize your impact if you allocated the full $100 to the highly effective charity. But that entails not giving anything to the charity of average effectiveness, something many participants were reluctant to do. Instead, they preferred to split their donations across the two charities. On a scale from 1 to 7, where 1 meant definitely choosing the splitting option and 7 meant definitely giving the full amount to the highly effective charity, the average response was 3.22 (Caviola, Schubert, & Nemirow, 2020).

Notably, even if we explained that giving the full amount to the most effective charity is the more effective option, a large fraction of participants continued to choose the splitting option (the average response was now 4.83 on the same scale, and a follow-up study gave convergent results). Also, remember the study from Chapter 2 where 44% of participants said that they wanted to split a $100 donation across two charities with different levels of effectiveness even when they were informed that the highly effective charity is 100 times more effective (Caviola, Schubert, Teperman, et al., 2020). These findings suggest that people are averse to fully deprioritizing less effective charities (Baron & Szymanska, 2011; Ubel et al., 1996a). Most people are fine with giving more to especially effective charities, but they still want to give something to less effective charities. They don't want to engage in the kind of single-minded triage that we tend to use in emergencies.

But though charity and emergencies are psychologically different, the logic of how to do the most good is just the same in both of them. Charitable donors have limited resources, just as the doctors in the Rwandan civil war had. If you decide to give money to a less effective charity, then you will have less money to give to a more effective charity. That entails, in turn, that your money will save fewer lives or otherwise do less good. The situation is perfectly analogous to that during the war in Rwanda, where those who would almost certainly die were deprioritized for the sake of those who had a decent chance to survive. As the effective altruist Holly Elmore (2016) puts it, "we are in triage every second of every day." But in spite of these similarities, people view charity and emergencies differently—since it's less salient that choosing to donate to a less effective charity leads to worse outcomes. Many keep giving some support to less effective charities even though that decreases their overall impact. This resistance to prioritization is one of the most powerful obstacles to helping effectively.

Deprioritizing some causes and some beneficiaries may appear cold. It may seem as if we don't care about them. This is probably a major reason that people are so averse to deprioritization. But deprioritization isn't cold or motivated by a lack of empathy. When we choose to deprioritize some patients in a triage situation, it's not because we don't care. It's not that we're not motivated to help those patients. Instead, our motivation is to help as much as possible—and it's hard to find a better or more caring motivation. It's true that a side effect of achieving that goal is that some people are deprioritized. But instead of narrowly focusing on this side effect, we should look at the aggregate outcome—at the total number of people we're able to save. Taking the steps that are needed to help as much as possible isn't in conflict with a caring motivation but rather the best way to express it.

The Lives We Could Have Saved

Let us look deeper into the psychological mechanisms that underpin the resistance to prioritize the most effective ways of helping. One such mechanism is *opportunity cost neglect* (Collett-Schmitt et al., 2015; Frederick et al., 2009; Maguire et al., 2023).

Whenever we buy a product, we forgo the opportunity to use that money to buy another product. Likewise, whenever we give to a charity, we forgo the opportunity to use that money to give to another charity. In that sense, buying a product or giving to a charity has an opportunity cost: the "cost" of not being able to take the best alternative opportunity. We often underestimate or neglect this opportunity cost. We don't adequately consider what else we could have done with our money—what other product we could have bought or what other charity we could have supported. As a result, we overestimate the value of the choices in front of us relative to less salient alternatives.

Opportunity cost neglect is a general phenomenon. For instance, it can lead consumers to overspend since they neglect what else they could have done with the money. But there are reasons to believe that we are particularly insensitive to opportunity costs when it comes to doing good. Consumers tend to be more motivated to get good value for money, which can make them more sensitive to opportunity costs. They think through their decisions more carefully and tend to compare multiple options when making a purchase—especially when it comes to large purchases such as a car or a house. The opportunity cost of buying a particular car or house—that they won't be able to buy any other cars or houses—is typically very salient to them. But people take a different approach when they're looking to do good. As we saw in Chapter 1, studies suggest only a small minority of donors research multiple charities (Camber Collective, 2015). Instead, many donors focus exclusively on a particular charity when deciding whether to donate or not. They neglect the possibility of donating to another charity. An archetypal situation may be a Facebook donation campaign, where the choice is between donating or not donating to the promoted charity and where alternative donation opportunities are not offered. As discussed in Chapter 2, people typically make charity decisions in separate evaluation ("Should I donate to this particular charity?") as opposed to joint evaluation ("Should I donate to this charity or that charity?"). This tendency to evaluate charities separately probably makes people more likely to neglect the opportunity cost of donating to less effective charities.

Alternative opportunities can be more or less salient. When they are more salient, we tend to neglect them less. In battlefield triage, the opportunity costs of failing to strictly prioritize the patients we have a greater chance of saving are staring us in the face. We see people dying with our own eyes. The costs of refusing to triage are highly salient. It becomes clear that not using all resources effectively leads to many more people dying. But in charity contexts, the opportunity costs of not prioritizing the most effective options are usually much less salient. The beneficiaries are far away and much less visible. The opportunity costs are, at best, numbers on paper—if they are recognized at all. And that can make us more inclined to neglect them (Caviola et al., 2021).

Trading off Sacred Values

Life is full of trade-offs. You might really like to go to that play at the theater on Friday, but you might also like to attend your favorite team's next home game. And you have limited money at the end of the month, so you have to choose. What is more important?

As consumers and investors, we are faced with these kinds of decisions all the time. They can sometimes feel tough. Under financial constraints, we may be forced to choose between things that are deeply meaningful to us. But still, we manage, by and large. We realize that we need to spend our resources sensibly and cannot have everything we want. We recognize that trade-offs are part and parcel of the human condition. So, we prioritize the things we care the most about. For instance, on reflection you may realize that the play is simply a bit more important for you. You want to go to the football game as well, but you know that you cannot have everything and need to prioritize.

The psychologist and political scientist Philip Tetlock calls humdrum, everyday things such as plays and football games *secular values* (Baron & Leshner, 2000; Baron & Spranca, 1997; Tetlock, 2003; Tetlock et al., 2000). Since we find it relatively straightforward to make trade-offs between different secular values, Tetlock calls such trade-offs *routine*. Most trade-offs between different goods and services are routine. Likewise, trading off money against goods or services tends to be routine.

But not all trade-offs are similarly routine. We are much less happy to make trade-offs that involve what Tetlock calls *sacred values*, such as human lives, religious and political values, and other things of special moral and emotional importance. In particular, we don't want to trade off sacred values (e.g., human lives) against secular values (e.g., money). Such trade-offs are viewed as *taboo*, in Tetlock's words (Tetlock, 2003). Just considering the idea of not spending money to save someone's life can elicit moral outrage and condemnation (Tetlock et al., 2000). People often think that a good person instantaneously should know that we always need to prioritize saving lives over saving money, no matter the costs.

And yet in order to help effectively, we sometimes should prioritize saving our money over saving lives. There may be other opportunities to use the money that would allow us to save more lives. If so, we need to save our money to be able to take those opportunities to help more effectively. But that really doesn't come naturally to us.

It may seem counterintuitive that we are less inclined to make trade-offs that involve sacred values. We care more about sacred values than about secular values since they carry a special significance for us. And if we care more about something, we should presumably be more interested in making sure we get as much as possible of it. We should be more interested in effectiveness—and since effectiveness entails making trade-offs, one might have thought that we would be particularly inclined to make trade-offs over sacred values. And yet the opposite is true. While we accept that we have to make trade-offs over secular values, we don't accept that when it comes to sacred values. When it comes to plays versus football games, we think, "since I slightly prefer the play over the game, I will prioritize the play, even though I would have enjoyed the football game as well." But most people don't take the same approach to choices involving human lives. They typically don't think "since I prefer to save more lives rather than fewer, I will deprioritize this less effective charity and save my money for higher-impact opportunities."

Instead, people often refuse to accept that giving to charity involves such trade-offs. They don't want to see that donating to a less effective charity means that they forgo the chance of saving more lives by giving to a more effective charity. Therefore, they try to avoid such prioritization decisions. They split their donations between multiple charities or stick with default options (e.g., with the charity they have always donated to), which may feel less like a decision than actively choosing another option.

But we cannot avoid making prioritization decisions. Sticking with our default option is still a decision—and often a less effective one. We have limited resources, and the world is filled with problems. Thus, we have to prioritize some problems and deprioritize others. The only thing we can influence is whether to make such prioritization decisions more or less effectively.

But, unfortunately, that is not the attitude we take to decisions involving sacred values. In fact, we are averse to prioritizing between sacred values not despite the fact that we care so much about them but precisely because we care so much about them. Human lives are so important to us that we feel that we cannot deprioritize anyone. Again, it is precisely the strength of our feelings that—tragically and ironically—misleads us. Just as our empathy leads us to be insensitive to the number of lives we could save (see Chapter 2), it also leads us to be averse to consistently prioritizing the most effective ways of helping.

And the solution is also the same. We should reorient our empathy, not reduce it. That we value human lives so highly is a powerful force for good. We should not get rid of this feeling, but we should channel it in more productive directions so that we save as many people as possible. We need to accept that to help as many as possible, we have to deprioritize some. It feels tough, but there is no other way.

Why Splitting Usually Isn't Effective

Aversion to trade-offs over sacred values is likely one reason people split their donations across multiple charities, but it isn't the only one. They also split simply because they believe that it is more effective. In the splitting study where we asked participants how they would allocate $100 across a highly effective charity and an average charity, we also asked participants which option they believe is most effective. We found that, on average, participants thought that splitting the donation across both charities would be roughly as effective as allocating the full amount to the highly effective charity (Caviola, Schubert, & Nemirow, 2020). Many thought that splitting is more effective.

At first glance, it may seem that splitting our donations should be effective. We are often advised to split or diversify our investments. And in many ways, it would be good if donors acquired more of an investor mindset since investors tend to be more focused on effectiveness. By that logic, shouldn't we diversify our donations, just like we diversify our investments?

While there are many similarities between how to donate and how to invest, the analogy breaks down in some ways. This is one such case. When we invest money for our own benefit, we typically prefer getting a certain sum for sure over having a 50% chance of getting twice as much and a 50% chance of getting nothing. Money has diminishing marginal utility: The more of it we have, the less valuable each additional dollar is. That means that we have reason to diversify our bets. There is typically a non-trivial risk that a given company goes bust, meaning that if we invest all our money in one company, we could lose it all. It's far less likely that 10 or 100 companies all go bust—so the more companies we invest in, the lower the risk, and the more stable the returns. That gives us reason to diversify our investments instead of going all in on one company.

But human lives don't have diminishing marginal benefits (Chapter 2). It is just as valuable to save a life, regardless of how many lives we've saved before. The 100th life that we save is no less valuable than the first. Therefore, saving a certain number of lives for sure is, in our view, not more (or less, for that matter) valuable than having a 50% chance of saving twice as many lives and a 50% chance of saving no lives. That means that the standard rationale for diversifying doesn't transfer from the investment domain to the donation domain. Instead, we normally have reason to concentrate our donations toward the most promising charity. While there is often a risk that they are not as effective as they seem, we should, in our view, accept that risk if it gives us the chance to have a sufficiently big impact. (Though there are some philosophers who think that, on the contrary, risk aversion can be warranted in altruistic contexts [see Chapter 5; Buchak, 2013, 2018].)

Another reason the analogy between investments and donations breaks down in this case is that the stock market is much more efficient than the charity "market" (Chapter 2). Since most investors are broadly rational, stock prices normally reflect companies' true values relatively well. Opportunities to get outsized returns on investments tend to get taken quickly, meaning it's hard to "beat the market." You rarely find opportunities that ensure you higher returns than the alternatives. Instead, the best you can do is usually to spread your bets across several companies and hope that some of them do especially well.

But the charity market is far less efficient. Donors are not effectiveness-minded and don't necessarily favor the most effective charities. That means opportunities to have an outsized impact won't necessarily be taken. Extraordinarily effective charities still have a *funding gap*—a lack of funds for useful projects—meaning donors can have an exceptionally high impact by filling that gap (Dalton, 2021). Therefore, it's usually more effective to concentrate your donations toward such a charity and refrain from splitting (Snowden, 2019).

There are, however, some cases where this is not true. Large donors may give so much that the most effective charity's funding gap is covered. For instance, suppose that the most effective available charity works on rolling out some medications in an area that is struck by disease. In that case, donations that would cover that particular medicine rollout are likely highly effective. But once that need is covered, the charity would need to pursue some other intervention with additional donations—and we may not know whether that intervention would be similarly effective. In such cases, it often makes sense for donors to redirect additional donations to the second-best charity. Large donors may reiterate this process—they go down the list of charities, filling their respective funding gaps one by one.

Thus, very large donors normally maximize their impact by splitting their donations since individual charities cannot fully absorb them. But for small donors giving a few thousand dollars or less, this is usually not an issue. The most effective charity will normally be able to use any small donations it receives toward high-impact programs. Therefore, small donors are usually better advised to give their whole donation to that charity. That is especially so since donations carry some overhead for charities: It costs some money and effort to process each donation. The overall processing costs will be lower if we just make one donation toward the most effective charity instead of splitting our donations across multiple charities.

So why do many people think it is more effective to split their donations across multiple charities? We already saw that one reason could be an erroneous analogy with investment diversification. But another possibility is that they may think that distributions of donations should correspond directly to charities' relative levels of effectiveness. According to this view, more effective charities should indeed receive more funding than less effective charities—but they shouldn't receive all of our donations. Instead, the less effective charity should receive a fraction of our donations in proportion to their level of effectiveness. If the more effective charity is twice as effective as the less effective charity, then this view says we should split our donation 67%/33%.

This way of thinking about donation effectiveness is intuitive but incorrect. To donate effectively, we need to "think on the margin," as economists say. We should look at how we would like to spend an additional or marginal dollar and ask, "Which charity would use this dollar most effectively, given all the other donations the charities have already received?" Once we have come to a decision, we ask the same question about the next dollar, and so on.

Let us look at what that method implies. Obviously, it says that we should give the first dollar to the most effective charity. What about the second dollar? Here we have to consider whether the marginal returns to additional donations diminish. As we've seen, they often do—since charities eventually tend to run out of high-impact projects to fund—but it doesn't happen that quickly. Therefore, the most effective charity will typically also use the second dollar more effectively than the less effective charity, and the third and the fourth dollars—and so on. Thus, this method says that the most effective charity will use all of the $100 more effectively than the less effective charity. Hence, it's more effective to give the full amount to the most effective charity.

This makes clear that our distribution of donations should not necessarily correspond with the relative effectiveness of different charities. Just because one charity is twice as effective as another, our donations shouldn't necessarily be split 67%/33%. Instead, it's typically better if small donors allocate their whole donations to the most effective charity (100%/0%).

Failure to think on the margin probably also underlies another fallacious argument for splitting: the so-called Kantian fallacy (Drescher, 2015). This argument is named after the philosopher Immanuel Kant, who famously argued that our behavior should be universalizable: that we should ask "What if everyone did that?" (Though note that there's no suggestion that Kant would actually have defended this argument—it's just a name.) In line with that, the argument says that we should not just prioritize the most effective charities, for what if everyone did that? The most effective charities would, according to this line of reasoning, end up with more money than they could productively spend, whereas less effective charities would receive no money at all. Thus, focusing our giving on the most effective charities would not increase the overall impact of donations but rather reduce it. Therefore, we're better off splitting our donations across multiple charities, the argument goes.

There are two problems with this argument. First, to be effective, we should look at the impact of our marginal dollars given what other donors actually do, not given what they hypothetically could do. It's true that most donors could switch to the most effective charities. It's also true that if they did, those charities would receive more money than they could productively spend. But realistically, that will not happen. It's unlikely that more than a small minority of donors will give to the most effective charities in the near future. Most people are not effectiveness-minded, and they're not going to change their ways suddenly. And given that most donors don't, in fact, give to the most effective charities, we maximize our impact by supporting those charities.

Second, even if effective giving became widely adopted, the potential problem that the Kantian fallacy points to would not arise. Insofar as effective donors are actually effective, they coordinate with each other to ensure that every additional donation is based on adequate information about other donations. If one donor fills the most effective charity's funding gap, other effective donors won't passively continue giving to that charity. Instead, they will reallocate their donations to another effective charity that still has a funding gap. The ordering of donation opportunities is not forever fixed but changes as the highest-impact opportunities are taken. Rational donors react dynamically to these changes and constantly re-evaluate how to maximize their impact. And they talk to each other: If one donor fills a charity's funding gap, they communicate that, allowing other donors to redirect their donations elsewhere. Thus, a community of effective donors wouldn't just support one or a small number of charities. Instead, they would support many charities. In fact, that's exactly what the effective altruism community does (Todd, 2023).

In conclusion, people overestimate the effectiveness of splitting and underestimate the value of concentrating donations toward the most effective charity. But this misconception is only part of the reason that people split donations across charities. As we've seen, they also simply have a preference for splitting (Caviola, Schubert, & Nemirow, 2020). Let's now dig deeper into where this preference for splitting comes from.

Prioritization and Fairness

We've already seen that aversion to trade-offs may contribute to the preference for splitting. People may see splitting as the least objectionable compromise in the face of an objectionable trade-off. Another reason for splitting could be that people experience diminishing marginal utility from giving more to the same charity (see the discussion on scope neglect in Chapter 2). Though $100 is 10 times more than $10, the subjective utility—the positive feeling—that they derive from donating $100 may not be 10 times greater than the subjective utility they derive from donating $10. Instead, the difference may be much smaller. That would mean that people derive much more utility from the first few dollars they give to a particular charity than from dollars they add to an already significant donation. And that would mean, in turn, that they derive more utility if they split their donations across multiple charities (see Chapter 6).

But another potential reason is that people may view it as fairer to split. They may find it unfair to give their whole donation to the most effective charity and nothing at all to other charities. In one study, Daron Sharps and Juliana Schroeder (2019) found that participants preferred to distribute donations equally across beneficiaries even when some of them had greater needs than others. This was motivated by procedural fairness as the participants felt it was fairer to give to everyone than to concentrate their donations toward one beneficiary.

A series of studies by Peter Ubel and his colleagues (1996b, 2001) give further evidence of how we often let equity and fairness considerations trump effectiveness. They asked participants to choose between two colon cancer screening tests which differed both in terms of their coverage and in terms of how many lives they saved. The first test would only screen half of the population but was estimated to save 1100 lives, whereas the second test would screen the whole population and save 1000 lives. Even though the first test would save more lives, most lay participants and even many experts in medical decision-making preferred the second test because they found it more equitable.

At first glance, it may seem like this is what fairness dictates. Choosing the first test entails that half of the population would be deprioritized, and that may seem unfair. Some may view it as similar to racism or sexism. But, in fact, it is wholly different. It is true that some people get deprioritized in the colon screening test case, but it's not because of any bias against them. Instead, it just so happens that it is more effective to help the smaller group. No one is discriminated against based on any personal characteristics. We prioritize the smaller group simply because we can help more people that way. That motivation is very different from racism, sexism, and other forms of unjustifiable discrimination.

People often think of fairness on the level of groups. The thought is, for example, that even if it is more effective to support arthritis research than cancer research, it would be unfair to the cancer patients to wholly deprioritize them in favor of the arthritis patients. But that doesn't seem to be the right way of looking at things. We should instead apply fairness to the level of individuals. We should try to help as many individuals as possible as much as possible, whether they suffer from arthritis, cancer, or whatnot. We should think, "Which individual could we help the most with a given sum of money?" If addressing a particular disease enables us to help more individuals, we should prioritize that disease. Not doing so would, in effect, be to value some people more just because they suffered from a disease that's more costly to treat. That seems neither effective nor fair.

Here is another way to see that. Suppose that we are allocating resources to patients suffering from two different diseases—say malaria and cancer—and that the malaria patients can be helped more effectively. We start out using cost-effectiveness principles and therefore prioritize malaria patients. After we've helped a number of malaria patients, we are considering whether we should treat a cancer patient or another malaria patient next. Would it be fairer to treat a cancer patient at this point, in order to split our efforts across the two patient groups? That doesn't seem to be the case. The untreated malaria patients don't benefit from other malaria patients having been treated. For each additional patient, it is irrelevant whether previously treated patients suffered from the same disease as them or from another disease (cf. the discussion on how every life matters equally in Chapter 2). All that matters is whether they get treated. And to maximize the number of cured patients, we need to prioritize the patients who can be helped more effectively on the margin. Our concern should be with concrete individuals, not with abstract groups.

In Chapter 3, we encountered the veil of ignorance: the philosophical thought experiment that asks what principles we would support if we didn't know who we are or what traits and assets we have. As you may recall, the idea is that such ignorance of our identity makes us more impartial and fair and more likely to make ethically correct decisions. Notably, studies have found that behind the veil of ignorance, where people don't know what medical conditions they are likely to have, they are more inclined to want hospitals to prioritize medical conditions that are more cost-effective to treat (since that maximizes chances of survival; Huang et al., 2019). This gives further support to the notion that there is nothing unfair about strictly prioritizing patients suffering from diseases that are more cost-effective to treat.

In our view, fairness considerations thus don't support splitting; and overall, small donors are often best advised to concentrate their donations toward one effective charity. We are aware that many people are reluctant to do that, however. Therefore, we discuss what you can do retain a relatively high level of effectiveness while splitting your donations across multiple charities in Chapter 9 (the *two-budget strategy*).

Conclusion

The need to prioritize some ways of doing good over others is emotionally challenging. It feels tough to deprioritize causes and beneficiaries that seem worthy of support. Intuitively, it cuts against the spirit of free generosity that, for many, is at the heart of altruism. It can feel cold and unfair—as if we don't care about those who cannot be helped as effectively as others. But nothing could be further from the truth. We want to help effectively exactly because we care strongly about everyone in need. And to do that, we unfortunately need to prioritize some and deprioritize others. Under scarce resources, there is no other way. To be effective, we have to accept this fact. We must overcome deprioritization aversion—one of the greatest obstacles to helping effectively.

References

Baron, J., & Leshner, S. (2000). How serious are expressions of protected values? *Journal of Experimental Psychology: Applied, 6*(3), 183–194.

Baron, J., & Spranca, M. (1997). Protected values. *Organizational Behavior and Human Decision Processes, 70*(1), 1–16.

Baron, J., & Szymanska, E. (2011). Heuristics and biases in charity. In D. M. Oppenheimer & C. Y. Olivola (Eds.), *The science of giving: Experimental approaches to the study of charity* (pp. 215–235). Psychology Press.

Buchak, L. (2013). *Risk and rationality.* Oxford University Press.

Buchak, L. (2018). Weighing the risks of climate change. *The Monist, 102*(1), 66–83.

Camber Collective. (2015). *Money for good 2015.*

Caviola, L., Schubert, S., & Mogensen, A. (2021). Should you save the more useful? The effect of generality on moral judgments about rescue and indirect effects. *Cognition, 206*, Article 104501.

Caviola, L., Schubert, S., & Nemirow, J. (2020). The many obstacles to effective giving. *Judgment and Decision Making, 15*(2), 159–172.

Caviola, L., Schubert, S., Teperman, E., Moss, D., Greenberg, S., & Faber, N. (2020). Donors vastly underestimate differences in charities' effectiveness. *Judgment and Decision Making, 15*(4), 509–516.

Collett-Schmitt, K., Guest, R., & Davies, P. (2015). Assessing student understanding of price and opportunity through a hybrid test instrument: An exploratory study. *Journal of Economics & Economic Education Research, 16*(1), 115–134.

Dalton, M. (2021, January 24). *Defining returns functions and funding gaps.* Centre for Effective Altruism. Retrieved January 27, 2024 from https://www.centreforeffectivealtruism.org/blog/defining-returns-functions-and-funding-gaps

Drescher, D. (2015, March 23). *Common misconceptions about effective altruism.* Effective Altruism Forum. https://forum.effectivealtruism.org/posts/fiGwaK7AAw9xLHcaw/common-misconceptions-about-effective-altruism

Elmore, H. (2016, August 26). We are in triage every second of every day. *Holly Elmore Blog.* https://mhollyelmoreblog.wordpress.com/2016/08/26/we-are-in-triage-every-second-of-every-day/
Frederick, S., Novemsky, N., Wang, J., Dhar, R., & Nowlis, S. (2009). Opportunity cost neglect. *The Journal of Consumer Research, 36*(4), 553–561.
Huang, K., Greene, J. D., & Bazerman, M. (2019). Veil-of-ignorance reasoning favors the greater good. *Proceedings of the National Academy of Sciences of the United States of America, 116*(48), 23989–23995.
MacAskill, W. (2015). *Doing good better: Effective altruism and a radical new way to make a difference.* Guardian Faber Publishing.
Maguire, A., Persson, E., & Tinghög, G. (2023). Opportunity cost neglect: A meta-analysis. *Journal of the Economic Science Association, 9,* 176–192.
McKie, J., & Richardson, J. (2011). Social preferences for the inclusion of indirect benefits in the evaluation of publicly funded health services: Results from an Australian survey. *Health Economics, Policy, and Law, 6*(4), 449–468.
Sharps, D. L., & Schroeder, J. (2019). The preference for distributed helping. *Journal of Personality and Social Psychology, 117*(5), 954–977.
Snowden, J. (2019). Should we give to more than one charity? In H. Greaves & T. Pummer (Eds.), *Effective altruism: Philosophical issues* (pp. 69–79). Oxford University Press.
Tetlock, P. E. (2003). Thinking the unthinkable: Sacred values and taboo cognitions. *Trends in Cognitive Sciences, 7*(7), 320–324.
Tetlock, P. E., Kristel, O. V., Elson, S. B., Green, M. C., & Lerner, J. S. (2000). The psychology of the unthinkable: Taboo trade-offs, forbidden base rates, and heretical counterfactuals. *Journal of Personality and Social Psychology, 78*(5), 853–870.
Todd, B. (2023, February). *Doing good together: How to coordinate effectively, and avoid single-player thinking.* 80,000 Hours. Retrieved January 27, 2024 from https://80000hours.org/articles/coordination/
Ubel, P. A., Baron, J., & Asch, D. A. (2001). Preference for equity as a framing effect. *Medical Decision Making, 21*(3), 180–189.
Ubel, P. A., DeKay, M., Baron, J., & Asch, D. A. (1996a). Public preferences for efficiency and racial equity in kidney transplant allocation decisions. *Transplantation Proceedings, 28*(5), 2997–3002.
Ubel, P. A., DeKay, M. L., Baron, J., & Asch, D. A. (1996b). Cost-effectiveness analysis in a setting of budget constraints—Is it equitable? *The New England Journal of Medicine, 334*(18), 1174–1177.

5
Misconceptions About Effectiveness

Throughout Part I, we've seen that most people have many misconceptions about how to be effective when doing good. Most people have never heard of the most effective charities (Chapter 1). They don't know that the most effective charities vastly outperform other charities, which leads them to underestimate the importance of finding those charities (Chapter 2). They don't know that it's usually more effective to help distant beneficiaries (Chapter 3). And they overrate the effectiveness of splitting their donations across charities (Chapter 4).

All of these misconceptions reduce our effectiveness when we're doing good. But another, and in some ways more fundamental, kind of misconception concerns the concept of effectiveness itself. In this chapter, we will look at a number of such conceptual misconceptions and see how they lower the effectiveness of people's altruistic efforts.

The Overhead Myth

Let us start by looking at what may be the most common misconception of this type: the so-called overhead myth regarding charity effectiveness. As we saw in Chapter 2, many donors associate charity effectiveness with low overhead costs—low costs for administration, fundraising, travel, and other forms of expenses not directly associated with the charity's programs. The thought is either that low overhead just is what it means for a charity to be effective or that low overhead is strongly correlated with a high level of effectiveness. But in fact, neither of those views is true. Research suggests that there is not much of a correlation at all between overhead and effectiveness (Berrett, 2020). A charity can be highly effective, for example, in the sense that it saves many lives per million dollars, even if it spends a substantial fraction on overhead.

Why is that? There are two main reasons. First, as we saw in Chapter 2, the most important determinants of charity effectiveness are the problem the charity has chosen to work on and the methods they employ to solve that problem. Those factors can give rise to 100-fold differences in effectiveness. Overhead ratios don't vary nearly as much: For example, charities with comparatively high salaries don't tend to pay 100 times higher salaries than the average charity. Thus, any differences in overhead tend to pale in comparison with differences in effectiveness related to choices of problem and method.

Second, though the discourse about charity overhead tends to be overwhelmingly negative, money spent on overhead isn't necessarily wasted. Charities often need to make investments that don't go directly toward their programs to be effective. Thus, unbeknownst to many donors, increasing overhead sometimes even increases effectiveness.

Some might think that even if low overhead isn't particularly correlated with high effectiveness, it's still valuable for its own sake. But it's hard to see that. Again, it helps to make an analogy with investments and consumption. When investors decide whether to buy stock in a company, they are not intrinsically interested in the company's salary costs and other overhead costs. Instead, they focus on how profitable the company is or can be expected to be. Similarly, consumers are not concerned with overhead. When deciding whether to buy some product, consumers are normally not directly interested in whether the producers' expenses could have been lower. Instead, their focus is on the quality and price of the product. Analogously, donors who aspire to be effective should focus on how much good the charity would do—for example, how many lives it would save—with their money, not on how much money would go to overhead.

However, in practice, overhead is a major concern for donors. In two studies we conducted with Jason Nemirow, we presented participants with one charity said to have low overhead costs and a medium level of cost-effectiveness and another charity said to have high overhead costs and a high level of cost-effectiveness. Even though it was thus explicitly said that the charity with high overhead has a higher level of cost-effectiveness, most participants said they would like to donate to the charity with low overhead (Caviola et al., 2020). On a scale from 1 to 7, where 1 meant definitely choosing the low-overhead charity and 7 meant definitely choosing the more effective charity, the average responses were 2.03 and 3.20 in the two studies.

And it's not just donors who are concerned with overhead. Media and even some third-party charity evaluators often focus more on overhead than on cost-effectiveness measures. This has started to change in recent years, with the charity evaluators GuideStar, Charity Navigator, and BBB Wise Giving

Alliance launching *The Overhead Myth* campaign in 2013 (Pallotta, 2013; QGiv, n.d.). However, Charity Watch, another charity evaluator, pushed back against this initiative, arguing that effectiveness is too hard to measure and that charity evaluators should continue to look at overhead (Charity Watch, 2014). Overall, it seems fair to say that overhead remains in focus in the charity sector.

Why, then, are people so focused on overhead? In part, the explanation is probably epistemic: Many people misunderstand the relationship between overhead and effectiveness, thinking they're much more tightly linked than they are. In the aforementioned study, we informed some participants that it is more effective to donate to the charity with high overhead costs and a high level of effectiveness than the charity with low overhead costs and a medium level of cost-effectiveness (see Chapter 6 for more details on the information we provided). These participants were much more likely to choose the more effective charity than participants who were not given such information and, on average, prioritized it (Caviola et al., 2020). This suggests that people look at overhead partly because they think it is identical to, or a good proxy for, effectiveness.

In part, this misconception may be due to a naive model of how charities work. This model would say that charity always involves directly transferring some basic resource such as food or medicine to the beneficiaries. Charities would purchase these resources for a fixed price per unit, and they would be roughly equally valuable to the beneficiaries. Under such a simplistic model, cost-effectiveness would indeed largely be a function of low overhead since there wouldn't be many other factors that could affect the charity's cost-effectiveness. Moreover, the difference in effectiveness between charities would typically be low since the difference in overhead is, as we've seen, realistically muted.

But, in fact, that is not how charities generally operate. Many charities don't just transfer basic resources but instead make far more complex interventions. They might, for instance, research the cause of a disease outbreak and then invest in infrastructure to stop the outbreak. These complex interventions have several features of interest for our purposes. First, they often require substantial overhead. Second, they often differ hugely in terms of effectiveness: As we've seen, some interventions are 100 times more effective than others. And third, it's often far harder to directly gauge their effectiveness than the transfer model suggests. To estimate the level of effectiveness, one often needs to engage in painstaking research. Few charities do that, and partly for that reason, they often end up employing interventions that are far from maximally effective. That's why the difference in effectiveness between charities is so large.

It is plausible that people focus on overhead in part precisely because it is easier to calculate and evaluate than cost-effectiveness. A charity's overhead ratio—costs for overhead divided by total costs—tends to be relatively straightforward to calculate. But to calculate cost-effectiveness, we need a measure of the charity's total impact (which we then divide by its total costs). As we will see in more detail later in this chapter, it's definitely possible to measure impact—but it is also harder to do in practice. That may make donors more inclined to focus on overhead.

Relatedly, it's often relatively easy to get an intuitive grasp of whether a given overhead ratio is small or large, whereas that's more difficult regarding cost-effectiveness numbers. We can intuitively grasp that an overhead ratio of more than 80%, say, is large, even if we don't know much about charity. It's relatively easy to get an intuitive sense of percentages since they have a lower (0%) and an upper (100%) bound. Also, people use percentages all the time in their daily life. By contrast, it's harder to get an intuitive sense of what we should count as a cost-effective charity. How many lives should we expect charities to save per million dollars? Should we expect them to save 10, 100, or 1000 lives? People are not used to this cost-effectiveness metric, and since it has no upper bound, it's much harder to intuitively grasp whether a particular number is small or large.

This problem is exacerbated by the fact that people often evaluate charities separately rather than jointly (Chapter 2). Most donors don't explicitly compare charities but instead evaluate them one by one. Since it's harder to evaluate things in separate evaluation, this practice favors criteria that are easier to evaluate, such as overhead. We can get an intuitive grasp of whether an overhead ratio is small or large even in separate evaluation, whereas that's much less true of cost-effectiveness.

A series of experiments by Lucius Caviola and some of his colleagues (2014) demonstrated this effect. The experiment featured two charities, which would use a $1000 donation as follows:

Charity A: Uses $600 (60%) toward overhead, and saves five lives with the remaining $400.
Charity B: Uses $50 (5%) toward overhead, and saves two lives with the remaining $950.

Participants were divided into three groups: one that only read about Charity A, one that only read about Charity B, and one that read about both charities. Thus, the first two groups were presented with the problem in separate evaluation, whereas the third was presented with it in joint evaluation. The participants were asked how they would distribute $1000: how much they would want to give to charity and how much they would want to keep for themselves. The third, joint-evaluation, group was also asked how much they wanted to give to Charity A and Charity B, respectively.

The findings were striking. In separate evaluation, participants collectively preferred Charity B, which had lower overhead. The group presented with Charity B wanted to donate more ($254) than the group presented with the more effective Charity A ($156). But in joint evaluation, this pattern was reversed: Participants who were presented with both charities on average wanted to donate more to the more effective Charity A ($310) than to the low-overhead Charity B ($102).

This is because participants who evaluate the charities jointly can directly compare their levels of cost-effectiveness. They can see that Charity A saves more lives than Charity B, even though it has higher overhead. Therefore, they want to donate more to Charity A—since most people ultimately want to save more lives. By contrast, separate-evaluation participants find it hard to evaluate the cost-effectiveness statistics. They can't tell whether saving two lives or five lives with $1000 is more or less than we should expect. On the other hand, they can tell that a 5% overhead ratio is low and that a 60% overhead ratio is high. Therefore, they're more influenced by those numbers. And as we've seen, in the real world, people typically evaluate charities one by one, in separate evaluation (Chapter 2). That makes them focus on the more evaluable overhead ratios rather than the less evaluable cost-effectiveness numbers. Thus, just as our tendency to evaluate charities separately contributes to scope neglect (Chapter 2), it also contributes to an exaggerated use of overhead ratios.

Overall, these findings suggest that the focus on overhead partially has epistemic causes. But it's probably not the whole story. In the studies where we pitted a charity with low overhead costs and a medium level of cost-effectiveness against a charity with high overhead costs and a high level of cost-effectiveness, we found that even though it made a difference to explain to participants that it is more effective to choose the latter, it didn't persuade everyone. On the scale from 1 to 7, where 1 meant definitely choosing the low-overhead charity and 7 meant definitely choosing the more effective charity, participants were only slightly more inclined to choose the more effective charity (4.80/4.48 in the two studies; Caviola et al., 2020).

Relatedly, we found evidence that people's beliefs about effectiveness come apart from their donation decisions. Participants' inclination to donate to the charity with low overhead and a medium level of cost-effectiveness was greater than their tendency to believe that it is more effective than the charity with high overhead and a high level of cost-effectiveness. This suggests that people have, to an extent, intrinsic preferences for low-overhead charities: what we may term *overhead aversion*. It may feel more satisfying to give directly to beneficiaries than to cover administration and salary costs. This preference may be similar to other donor preferences, such as the preference for identifiable victims over larger numbers of statistical victims (Chapter 2; Duncan, 2004). Donors generally prefer salient and concrete forms of impact over more indirect and abstract forms of impact.

Another possibility is that people prefer low-overhead charities because they think they're less likely to be wasteful and corrupt (Chapter 1). They may hold a special aversion to waste and corruption, making them willing to pay a price in terms of reduced effectiveness to ensure that no part of their donations is lost in that way. In effect, they might consider it a sacred value (Chapter 4) not to fund wasteful and corrupt charities—and, as we've seen, people don't want to compromise over sacred values. These sentiments may be fueled by media outrages over charities that are perceived as overspending on salaries and other expenses. It is clearly a topic that many feel strongly about. Donors don't want to feel fooled.

The strong focus on overhead has several negative effects on the charity sector. First, it probably leads to less money going to the most effective charities. If we use a criterion that's not a good proxy for effectiveness, it's unlikely that our donations will be effective. But, second, it also gives charities the wrong incentives. It encourages them to save on overhead instead of increasing their effectiveness. Some charities report that they have cut down on expenses that would increase their cost-effectiveness for fear of being seen as having too high overhead costs. The Nonprofit Overhead Cost Study found that the focus on low overhead leads to a "nonprofit starvation cycle," with "nonfunctioning computers, staff members who lack the training needed for their positions, and, in one instance, furniture so old and beaten down that the movers refused to move it" (Gregory & Howard, 2009; Wing et al., 2004). Clearly, it is much better if charities can make the investments they need to do their work effectively without fearing the loss of funding.

Direct Versus Indirect Impact

We saw that people might be biased against charities with high overhead partly because they prefer to have a direct impact, where the causal chain between them and the ultimate beneficiaries is short and obvious. This suggests that overhead aversion may in part be a special case of a more general bias against more indirect forms of impact.

Lucius Caviola tested this hypothesis of a general indirectness aversion in a study he conducted with Joshua Lewis (2021). They informed participants that they could either donate directly to their favorite charity or support a company that fundraises for that charity. The fundraising company was said to employ professional fundraisers with a strong track record. If a participant gave the fundraising company $1, it would raise $10 for the charity. Participants could thus expect to have a 10 times larger impact if they allocated their money to the fundraising company rather than directly to their favorite charity. This logic was spelled out to the participants, and thus it was made clear that they would have a larger (albeit more indirect) impact if they chose to support the fundraising company. Despite that, Caviola and Lewis found that only half of the participants chose to support the fundraising company, while the other half preferred donating directly to their favorite charity.

This supports the hypothesis that many people prioritize interventions with a more direct path to impact, even when informed that they're less effective. There are several possible explanations for this. In this study, some participants were skeptical that it would indeed be more effective to support the fundraising company. Thus, beliefs about the effectiveness of indirect paths to impact likely play a role. However, it's also plausible that people have an intrinsic aversion to paying a fundraising company. Moreover, it's possible that these two factors are related: that people underestimate indirect impact precisely because they have an intrinsic aversion to it (i.e., that they engage in motivated reasoning).

We see yet again that people think differently about for-profits and charities. Suppose that an investor was told that they could either invest in a moderately profitable company that produces goods and services or in a more profitable investment company that invests in other companies that, in turn, produce goods and services. Most people would likely prefer the investment company, even though it earns its profits more indirectly. When we invest, what counts is the size of the profit, not whether the companies in question directly produce goods and services or invest in other companies that do. But donors take a different approach.

The preference for a more direct impact may also lead people to prefer volunteering over donations. It's often more effective to spend additional hours at your regular job and donate part of your extra income than to spend the same amount of time volunteering (Chapter 9). It can be hard to be highly effective at a task you're just spending a few hours a week on (Todd, 2020). And yet, people often prefer volunteering over donating money. This may at least in part be because it feels like you're having a more direct impact when you volunteer than when you donate (Kassirer & Touré-Tillery, 2023).

Biases against indirect impact can be a crucial obstacle to effective altruism because some charities with highly indirect impact have been estimated to be very effective. One example is what effective altruists call *meta-charities*: charities that have an impact via other charities. There are several types of meta-charities. One type is fundraising charities (cf., the fundraising company we just discussed), which can multiply the impact of your donations by raising more money than they consume. For instance, High Impact Athletes encourages elite athletes to donate part of their income to effective charities. Another example is Giving What We Can, a giving community whose members commit to give away 10% of their income to highly effective charities. A third is The Life You Can Save, which is inspired by Peter Singer's eponymous book. These meta-charities are estimated to be highly effective. High Impact Athletes (2022) reports a so-called multiplier effect of more than 2:1, meaning that every dollar they received is associated with more than $2 to another effective charity. Giving What We Can (Townsend & Hoeijmakers, 2023) estimates that it has a 30:1 multiplier effect, whereas The Life You Can Save (n.d.) reports a 15:1 multiplier effect (though differences in methodology mean that these numbers aren't necessarily directly comparable).

Other meta-charities take an even more indirect approach. Instead of fundraising for specific effective charities directly, they evaluate charities in terms of effectiveness and make recommendations to donors. The previously mentioned GiveWell is the best-known charity evaluator that uses effective altruist principles (Chapters 1 and 3). GiveWell evaluates charities that help the global poor and recommends a small set of particularly effective charities. GiveWell and other charity evaluators play a crucial role as they help effectiveness-minded donors to allocate their money as effectively as possible. Thus, it's essential not to refrain from giving to charity evaluators just because their impact is less direct.

Can We Compare Different Causes?

So far, we've seen that people have misconceptions about effectiveness related to overhead and indirect impact. But people also have other misconceptions about effectiveness in altruistic contexts. A key misconception is that we can't compare the impact of work on different altruistic causes (Caviola et al., 2021; Hsieh & Andersson, 2021). According to this view, we cannot, for instance, compare the effectiveness of charities focused on cancer (a frequently life-threatening disease) with charities focused on arthritis (a disease that mostly affects the quality of life). And cancer charities are still less comparable, according to this argument, with charities that focus on art, education, or other non-health causes. This view leads many to reject claims that a particular way of doing good is more effective than another. Consequently, they continue to support less effective causes.

This is another way people treat altruistic efforts differently from for-profit investments. Investors routinely compare for-profit companies that work on totally different issues: health care, education, energy, finance, and so on. They are not worried about these companies being incomparable. Though they operate in very different industries, one can still compare them in terms of expected return on investment (Berman et al., 2018). Investors thus have a common currency that they use to compare very different kinds of companies.

But many people take a different view of charity and other forms of altruistic efforts. They think that we don't have an analogous common currency for altruistic efforts and that we therefore can't compare different causes, such as health care, art, and education. Instead, do-gooders must choose causes in some other way—e.g., using their subjective preferences—, according to this reasoning.

But, in fact, there are common currencies for altruistic efforts as well. Economists have developed sophisticated cost-effectiveness metrics, which we can use to compare altruistic efforts focused on very different causes. A preliminary approach is, as we've seen, to measure effectiveness in terms of the number of lives we can save with a given amount of resources (Chapter 2). That could give us a common currency for comparing altruistic efforts directed toward all kinds of causes.

However, while this definition is a good first stab, it obviously doesn't work in all cases. For one thing, many altruistic efforts are not aiming to save lives but have very different goals. We thus need a more general definition. Let's first look at a definition that allows us to compare the cost-effectiveness of all sorts of medical interventions before we turn to an even more general measure.

Quality-Adjusted Life Years

Defining the cost-effectiveness of medical interventions in terms of saved lives has two problems. First, we want to distinguish between life-saving interventions that extend someone's life span by, say, 1 year and life-saving interventions that extend their life span by, say, 50 years. Clearly, the second class of interventions is more valuable. Second, some medical interventions help people by improving the quality of their lives rather than by extending them. Curing someone from a painful disease is obviously very valuable, even if it doesn't make them live longer. We want a measure that allows us to compare such interventions' levels of effectiveness with those of life-extending interventions.

Health economists have developed measures intended to do just that, such as the quality-adjusted life years (QALYs) metric. As briefly discussed in Chapter 2, a QALY is a year of someone's life adjusted for its quality (Banerjee & Duflo, 2011; Zeckhauser & Shepard, 1976). These quality adjustments are usually determined via surveys of patients having the disease in question. They are asked how many years with the disease they would trade for 1 year of life in full health. For instance, if they claim that they would trade 2 years of life with a disease causing severe pain for 1 year of life in full health, then 1 year with such a disease is worth 0.5 QALYs.

Using QALYs, we can compare the effectiveness of interventions that cure people of such a painful disease with interventions that save people's lives. Suppose, for instance, that an intervention would cure a patient from such a disease at a cost of $10,000 and that their life span after the cure would be 40 years (Figure 5.1). This would mean that the intervention saves 20 QALYs (40 × 0.5) with $10,000 (i.e., 2 QALYs/$1000). Suppose also that another intervention could save the life of another patient, who suffers from another disease, with $10,000. If their life were saved, they would go on to live for 10 years, meaning that that intervention saves 10 QALYs with $10,000 (i.e., 1

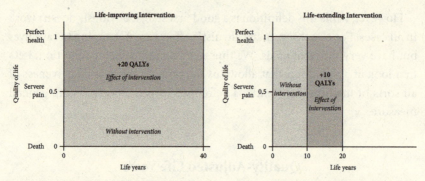

Figure 5.1 Additional Quality-Adjusted Life Years (QALYs) Resulting From Two Interventions

Note: The life-improving intervention (left) improves the quality of a person's life from 0.5 to 1. This saves more QALYs (40 years × 0.5 = 20) than the life-extending intervention (right), which extends a person's life by 10 years (10 years × 1 = 10).

QALY/$1000). In this example, the intervention that cures a life-saving disease would thus be less effective than the intervention that cures a disease causing severe pain.

In this way, we can use QALYs/$1000 as a common currency for comparing the effectiveness of medical interventions that save lives with those that improve other health-related outcomes. We can use this measure to compare interventions that address totally different diseases, such as HIV and malaria or arthritis and cancer. We just estimate how much longer and better patients' lives become thanks to the treatment and divide by how much it costs.

Well-Being-Adjusted Life Years

QALYs/$1000 is a widely used measure in healthcare prioritization. It's a very useful measure, but an obvious limitation is that it only measures the effectiveness of health-related interventions. Many altruistic efforts are not aimed at improving health but rather focus on art, education, the environment, or other valuable causes. We thus need a more general metric of effectiveness that can allow us to compare all sorts of causes and interventions.

A popular suggestion is the well-being-adjusted life year (WELLBY) metric (Layard & Oparina, 2021). It is a generalization of the QALY measure that is defined in terms of an intervention's overall effects on well-being instead of just their health-related effects. Well-being can, in turn, be measured in several ways: for example, in terms of subjective happiness (how happy or sad we feel, our "hedonic state"), in terms of preference satisfaction (whether our desires come true or not), or in terms of an "objective list" (containing goods seen as objectively valuable, like knowledge and freedom; Crisp, 2021). Which of these measures to choose is a complex issue which we cannot discuss in detail here, but for convenience we will focus on the conceptually straightforward hedonist theory. It allows us to measure WELLBYs similarly to QALYs: For example, one can survey people about how happy they are at different points in time and try to establish the causal effects of particular interventions. This means that one can compare altruistic efforts that address all kinds of problems. For instance, we can compare cancer charities with charities focusing on education. (Though some philosophers find certain kinds of comparisons objectionable or otherwise infeasible [Richardson, 1994; Sinnott-Armstrong, 1985].)

We should also note that there is considerable convergence between the hedonist theory and alternative theories. For instance, philosophers and other experts who value other things besides happiness (like knowledge or freedom) also tend to put substantial moral weight on happiness. That means that, in many cases, proponents of the different theories of well-being will rank causes and interventions similarly.

But there are also other ethical issues of relevance for how to measure effectiveness besides which fundamental metric to use. One key question is what weight we should put on the well-being of different beneficiaries: for example, whether we should put more weight on the well-being of the worst off. We use the simplest metric—WELLBY maximization. This metric gives the same weight to everyone's well-being, regardless of how much well-being they already have. Egalitarian-minded philosophers think that we rather should put additional weight on the well-being of the worst off, even at the possible expense of total well-being (Arneson, 2022; Hirose, 2014). However, in practice, there is substantial convergence between these metrics since we can often maximize the total amount of well-being by helping the worst off (Halstead et al., 2021). Diminishing marginal returns of money on happiness means that spending on the worst off is in many (but not all) cases a cost-effective way of maximizing total well-being.

A related issue is how much moral weight we should put on the well-being of different kinds of individuals. How much weight should we, for instance, put on the well-being of animals (Fischer, 2022; Muehlhauser, 2018; Sebo, 2022)? And how much should we value the well-being of future people? As we saw in Chapter 3, several difficult philosophical questions bear on that issue, including what the moral value of bringing a person into existence is (Broome, 2004; Greaves, 2017; Narveson, 1973; Rabinowicz, 2009). How we resolve these ethical issues can have profound implications for effective altruist prioritization, given how many animals there are and how many future people may come to exist.

Thus, while the WELLBYs/$1000 metric is conceptually straightforward, it is often hard to measure the effectiveness of altruistic interventions in practice. Even expert researchers are often very uncertain about how effective particular interventions are. One source of uncertainty is moral uncertainty over what theory of well-being to adopt, what weight to put on different beneficiaries' well-being, and so on (MacAskill et al., 2020). Another is the sheer difficulty of measuring individuals' levels of well-being and comparing them with each other (Harsanyi, 1990; Hausman, 1995). A still further issue is that it's often difficult to determine the causal effect of our interventions. We often don't know whether to attribute changes to our own interventions or to other factors that are unrelated to our work. When you're assessing your impact, you need to look at what would have happened if it weren't for your actions: that is, what counterfactual difference you made. For instance, individual donations to a charity sometimes make less of a difference than it naively seems since the charity's funding needs would have been covered by another donor if it weren't for your donation. These issues can make assessments of your counterfactual impact bewilderingly complex (Todd, 2021).

The fact that we can't just look at the direct effects of our interventions but must also look at various indirect effects can increase uncertainty further. For instance, it has been argued that deworming programs curing children of parasites indirectly improve educational outcomes since they allow children to return to school (Davey et al., 2015; Hamory et al., 2021; Miguel & Kremer, 2004). Since such potential indirect effects often are hard to assess, they tend to make our estimates even more uncertain.

Objections to Cross-Cause Comparability

Sheer lack of awareness of metrics like QALYs and WELLBYs is probably a key reason that many people think we cannot compare the effectiveness of efforts addressed toward different causes. But there may also be an argument from rigor, saying that if we are sufficiently uncertain, then we should abstain from making claims about the relative effectiveness of different causes. According to this line of thinking, it is epistemically irresponsible to make such claims when we don't have relatively strong evidence. Instead, the right approach is to suspend judgment (Grace, 2010).

In addition to these epistemic reasons, people may have an intrinsic aversion to cross-cause comparisons. In Chapter 4, we saw that many people are averse to trade-offs: that they dislike having to deprioritize some causes for the sake of others. Since we need to compare to prioritize, people who don't want to prioritize have a motive not to compare. And that motive not to compare may influence their beliefs about the comparability of different causes. In this way, unwillingness to prioritize between causes may lead people to believe that it's impossible to compare them.

The view that we can't, or shouldn't, compare different causes thus seems to come naturally to many people. But in our view, we have no choice but to compare causes and prioritize between them, including when the evidence is weak. To see that, let us make an analogy between cause prioritization and decisions in our personal lives. Suppose we are lost in the woods without a mobile phone, and it is getting late. Suddenly, the path diverges into two, and we have to make a critical decision. We have some slight evidence that one path is better. Maybe it is at least initially going slightly upward, and we know that our destination is at a higher altitude. Obviously, this is very weak evidence, and yet it seems wrong to ignore it and just flip a coin. Given the importance of the decision, we want to use whatever evidence we have to get it right.

The same is true of cause prioritization. Even if our evidence is weak and uncertain, we should use it and not throw it away. We should hang on to every means of increasing our chances of getting it right. We should acknowledge uncertainty, but we shouldn't refrain from making informed guesses.

Moreover, the large differences in effectiveness between altruistic interventions (Chapter 2) are to our advantage. If the differences had been small, then small errors in our estimates of effectiveness would have led us to get the relative effectiveness of different interventions wrong. Such errors would have led us to support less effective interventions over more effective interventions. But since the differences in effectiveness are in fact large, we can get the relative estimates right even if our estimates of the interventions' absolute levels of effectiveness are somewhat off. For example, suppose we're comparing a charity that supports sports facilities at American universities with a charity that distributes bed nets against malaria in a developing country. Even though it's very hard to estimate their respective levels of effectiveness precisely, the fact that interventions and causes differ so much in effectiveness means that it is likely that the malaria charity generates more WELLBYs/$1000 than the sports facilities charity even under very conservative assumptions. While this example may seem contrived, the same type of reasoning applies more generally to many kinds of charity and cross-cause comparisons.

Aversion to Risky Giving

Uncertainty about intervention effectiveness can make people averse to necessary cross-cause comparisons, but it can also make their altruistic efforts less effective in another way. Many are averse to interventions whose impact is uncertain, even if those interventions are otherwise promising. Instead, they prefer having some level of impact for sure. They are, in that sense, risk-averse. This is another important obstacle to effective altruism.

As we saw in Chapter 4, the analogy between investing and altruistic efforts breaks down when it comes to risk. Investors are naturally risk-averse since additional money tends to have diminishing returns for them. But donors and other do-gooders should, in our view, not be risk-averse since there aren't diminishing returns to WELLBYs or to saving lives. Instead, they should be "risk-neutral"—they should be neutral between the following options (Chapter 4):

Option 1: Saving x WELLBYs for sure.
Option 2: A 50% chance of saving $2x$ WELLBYs and a 50% chance of saving no WELLBYs.

In other words, they should maximize what is called *expected value* or *expected WELLBYs*: the value that our interventions are predicted or expected to have on average. This is a key concept in effective altruism (as well as in decision theory and economics; Steele & Stéfansson, 2020; Effective Altruism Forum, n.d.).

The expected value of an intervention is calculated as follows. First, we need to identify all the potential outcomes of the intervention. Let's create a toy example and keep things simple by assuming that the only relevant outcomes are saved lives. Suppose that we think that our intervention has three potential outcomes: no saved lives, one saved life, or two saved lives. Next, we need to estimate how likely the three outcomes are and multiply the likelihood of each outcome by how valuable it would be. For instance, if there is a 30% chance that our intervention will save one life, then that outcome generates 0.3 expected lives. Lastly, we add up these expected lives. Say there is a 40% chance that our intervention will save no lives and a 30% chance that it will save two lives. In that case, our intervention will save $(0.4 \times 0) + (0.3 \times 1) + (0.3 \times 2) = 0.9$ expected lives.

But while expected value maximization is, in our view, the normatively correct approach to decision-making under uncertainty, people often deviate from it. In a study on risky giving, we asked participants which of two charities, Charity A and Charity B, they would give $1000 (Caviola et al., 2020) to. Charity A was said to "use a technique that is proven to work every time. Each $1000 donated will save one life with 100% chance." On the other hand, Charity B was said to use "a more experimental technique that can be extremely effective but doesn't work every time. Each $1000 donated will save 100 lives with 10% chance, and 0 lives with 90% chance." Since Charity A saves one life in expectation, whereas Charity B saves 10 lives in expectation ($[0.1 \times 100] + [0.9 \times 0]$), the way to maximize expected value is clearly to donate to Charity B. And yet donors tended to choose Charity A, which saves one life for sure.

We also included an additional condition, where we informed participants that it is more effective to donate to Charity B since it saves more lives in expectation. These participants were more likely than participants who hadn't been thus informed to prioritize Charity B, but on average, they were torn between the two charities. In other words, they didn't clearly prefer the charity with the higher expected impact even after we explained to them that it is more effective to do so. These results suggest that both preferences and beliefs contribute to people's tendency to prioritize charities that have lower impact for sure over charities with higher but more uncertain expected impact. Part of the problem is that people genuinely believe that the former are more effective, but another issue is that they to an extent simply prefer such charities.

As mentioned in Chapter 4, we should point out, however, that some philosophers argue that we should sometimes be risk-averse when we're making decisions to help others (Buchak, 2013, 2018). This is a complex debate we can't do justice to here, but it should be noted that since Charity B has so much higher expected value than Charity A in the study we just covered, individuals who are merely moderately (as opposed to extremely) risk-averse would presumably choose Charity B. The claim that people can be excessively risk-averse in altruistic contexts thus does not stand and fall with risk-neutrality being normatively correct.

Excessive risk aversion can lower our impact substantially since many of the most impactful projects involve a risk of low or no impact (Karnofsky, 2016). For instance, this is true of many interventions involving potentially valuable new technologies. The dissemination of high-yield crop varieties during the Green Revolution was crucial for the food security of many developing countries (Jain, 2010). Today, clean technologies promise to play a major part in the battle against climate change (Gates, 2021; Halstead, 2018). But investing in new technology tends to be risky since there is always the chance that our plans will come to naught. Thus, if we are overly risk-averse, we won't support them, even if their expected impact is very large. This means that it is important not to be excessively risk-averse when we're trying to do good.

The Growing Effectiveness Gap

Throughout this chapter, we've seen that people have a range of conceptual misconceptions about effectiveness in the altruistic domain. In addition, they have several purely factual misconceptions about which charities are most effective and what types they belong to (Chapters 1 and 3). These misconceptions are striking since investors and consumers don't tend to have analogous misconceptions to nearly the same extent. For instance, investors tend to know how to compare investments in very different companies. They know that we can just look at profits or expected returns on investment. Why don't people have corresponding forms of knowledge about their altruistic efforts? Why don't they learn how to be more effective?

One reason is probably that effectiveness in the altruistic domain is a relatively abstract concept. Profit is a more tangible metric: It is measured in terms of money, which we are all habituated to from a young age. By contrast, it is not intuitively obvious how to compare altruistic efforts focused on different causes.

But another reason is probably that donors and other do-gooders simply aren't as interested in effectiveness as investors are. As we saw in Chapter 1, this lack of interest in effectiveness causes donors to abstain from searching for the most effective charities. It also likely contributes to all sorts of other misconceptions. For instance, it is likely part of the reason that people have a poor understanding of what effectiveness means in the altruistic domain. They are simply not sufficiently motivated to learn about it. By contrast, investors are much more interested in effectiveness, and therefore try harder to understand how to measure and compare different sorts of investments.

In this way, differential motivations directly contribute to our altruistic efforts being less effective than our investment decisions: what we may term the *effectiveness gap*. But this is not the only way differential motivations contribute to the effectiveness gap. Over the years, investors have built many tools in the pursuit of profit: tools that make it easier to be an effective investor. They include the joint stock company, stock exchanges, index funds, various instruments for borrowing and lending money, and many others. Likewise, knowledge of how to best use these different instruments has become diffused in society, and thus readily available for individual investors. Moreover, biases against specific financial instruments have gradually been worn down. In the Middle Ages, there was widespread opposition to taking interest on loans in Europe (Adamo et al., 2018). This norm was likely harmful since it reduced lending, including to highly productive projects. (People have little reason to put their money at risk by lending it to strangers if they can't charge interest.) But the norm against interest gradually disappeared, likely in part because people realized how economically beneficial a well-functioning lending market is.

Thus, investors' inclination to maximize profits dispels biases, misconceptions, and economically harmful norms in multiple ways. First, it increases the chance that an individual investor will overcome those biases, misconceptions, and norms and acquire any available knowledge about how to maximize profits. But, second, it also creates positive externalities for other investors and makes it easier for them to maximize their profits. Because investors down through the ages have wanted to maximize profits, they have built tools like stock exchanges and index funds; and similarly, they have rejected economically harmful norms, such as the norm against interest-taking. In effect, they have created a cultivated economic landscape where profit maximization is much easier than it once was, including for people who don't work hard to maximize profits. These days, people who save for retirement can just log in to their internet bank and get a lot of useful information about stock performance and how to maximize returns. Features like those were created because profit-maximizing investors demanded them. Thus, even a lazy investor can do relatively well today, thanks to other people's interest in maximizing the returns on their investments.

But in charity, people don't have the same interest in maximizing effectiveness, and therefore people haven't developed tools conducive to effectiveness to nearly the same extent. Measures of effectiveness such as QALYs/$1000 and WELLBYs/$1000 were only developed relatively recently, and information about them isn't nearly as widely disseminated as information about how to profit from investments. Banks certainly don't provide donors with tools and information to maximize the impact of their donations, the way they provide investors with tools and information to maximize their returns on investment.

Similarly, whereas many norms that reduce profits and returns on investments (such as the norm against interest-taking) have disappeared, the same is not true of norms that reduce the effectiveness of charitable giving and other altruistic efforts. A salient case is the norm against high overhead, which has many similarities with the norm against interest-taking. Interest and overhead are both relatively indirect expenditures—they are one step removed from tangible outputs—which people can be suspicious of. Another similarity is that both norms reduce effectiveness in their respective domains. But whereas the norm against interest-taking has largely disappeared, there is still very much a norm against high overhead. That is likely in part because donors have a relatively weak interest in maximizing effectiveness, whereas investors have a strong interest in maximizing returns on investment.

Thus, the effectiveness gap between investments and altruistic efforts has likely grown over the years. Investors have sought to maximize their returns, leading them to create new tools and norms conducive to greater returns. That, in turn, helped other investors maximize their returns. In this way, profit-maximizing carried positive externalities for other investors. But because do-gooders haven't been similarly interested in maximizing the effectiveness of their altruistic efforts, they haven't developed similar tools and norms in the altruistic domain—and so haven't generated such positive externalities for other do-gooders. This has widened the effectiveness gap.

Investors' and consumers' strong interest in getting the most value for money also creates another positive externality. Recall that we showed in Chapter 2 that prices for similar consumer goods and services tend to be driven into a fairly narrow range. Companies that offer much higher prices for the same or similar products won't be able to survive. Similarly, the prices of shares in overvalued companies tend to decrease since investors don't want to buy them. As a result, it is usually relatively easy to get decent value for money as an investor or consumer. There simply aren't that many substandard offers around. That means that while you may not get the absolute best value for money without extensive research, you usually get something that is not hugely worse.

By contrast, getting decent value for money as a donor is not easy. Since donors are much less focused on effectiveness, charities aren't driven into a narrow effectiveness range. Instead, most charities are much less effective than the most effective charities. Unless you put in the work to find those highly effective charities, your donations will likely be much less effective than they could have been (Chapter 2).

Thus, a number of different externalities increase the effectiveness gap between investment and consumption decisions, on the one hand, and altruistic efforts, on the other. In one sense, that's bad news—but there is also a positive side. In Part II, we will look at what we can do to increase people's focus on effectiveness in the altruistic domain. That is obviously a hard task. But it follows from the above reasoning that even if only some people became more focused on effectiveness in the altruistic domain, their work could increase everyone else's effectiveness as well. These effectiveness-minded do-gooders can, for instance, build sites that provide advice on which careers (80,000 Hours) or donations (e.g., GiveWell) are most effective; and other do-gooders could then use those sites to become more effective. Thus, while externalities have so far widened the effectiveness gap, they may also help us to close it.

Conclusion

In this chapter, we have seen that many people have a range of conceptual misconceptions about effectiveness in the altruistic domain. They tend to confuse the overhead ratio with charity effectiveness. They tend to underestimate risky projects because they don't grasp the concept of expected value. And they don't know that we can measure and compare the effectiveness of work on different causes. All of these misconceptions contribute to the fact that our altruistic efforts tend to be much less effective than they could be.

With that, we conclude Part I. We have seen that there are many psychological obstacles to effective altruism. First, people have a range of preferences that reduce the effectiveness of their help. They include preferences for charities they have a personal connection with (Chapter 1), preferences for supporting proximate rather than distant beneficiaries (Chapter 3), and an aversion to making uncomfortable trade-offs required to maximize effectiveness (Chapter 4). Second, people hold various incorrect beliefs that reduce the effectiveness of their efforts further. They include ignorance of what the most effective charities are (Chapter 1) as well as misconceptions about the differences in effectiveness between different altruistic efforts (Chapter 2) and misconceptions about what effectiveness is (Chapter 5).

Let us now turn to how these obstacles can be overcome.

References

Adamo, S., Alexander, D., & Fasiello, R. (2018). Usury and credit practices in the Middle Ages. *Contabilità E Cultura Aziendale, 1*, 37–69.

Arneson, R. J. (2022). *Prioritarianism.* Cambridge University Press.

Banerjee, A. V., & Duflo, E. (2011). *Poor economics: A radical rethinking of the way to fight global poverty.* PublicAffairs.

Berman, J. Z., Barasch, A., Levine, E. E., & Small, D. A. (2018). Impediments to effective altruism: The role of subjective preferences in charitable giving. *Psychological Science, 29*(5), 834–844.

Berrett, J. L. (2020). *Burying the overhead myth and breaking the nonprofit starvation cycle: Identifying more valid measures and determinants of nonprofit efficiency* [Unpublished doctoral dissertation]. North Carolina State University.

Broome, J. (2004). *Weighing lives.* Oxford University Press.

Buchak, L. (2013). *Risk and rationality.* Oxford University Press.

Buchak, L. (2018). Weighing the risks of climate change. *The Monist, 102*(1), 66–83.

Caviola, L., Faulmüller, N., Everett, J. A. C., Savulescu, J., & Kahane, G. (2014). The evaluability bias in charitable giving: Saving administration costs or saving lives? *Judgment and Decision Making, 9*(4), 303–316.

Caviola, L., & Lewis, J. (2021). *Indirectness aversion in charitable giving* [Unpublished manuscript]. Department of Psychology, Harvard University.

Caviola, L., Schubert, S., & Greene, J. D. (2021). The psychology of (in)effective altruism. *Trends in Cognitive Sciences, 25*(7), 596–607.

Caviola, L., Schubert, S., & Nemirow, J. (2020). The many obstacles to effective giving. *Judgment and Decision Making, 15*(2), 159–172.

Charity Watch. (2014, June 2). *Overhead ratios are essential for informed giving.* Retrieved January 27, 2024 from https://www.charitywatch.org/charity-donating-articles/overhead-ratios-are-essential-for-informed-giving

Crisp, R. (2021, September 15). Well-being. In E. N. Zalta (Ed.), *Stanford encyclopedia of philosophy* (winter 2021 ed.). https://plato.stanford.edu/entries/well-being/

Davey, C., Aiken, A. M., Hayes, R. J., & Hargreaves, J. R. (2015). Re-analysis of health and educational impacts of a school-based deworming programme in western Kenya: A statistical replication of a cluster quasi-randomized stepped-wedge trial. *International Journal of Epidemiology, 44*(5), 1581–1592.

Duncan, B. (2004). A theory of impact philanthropy. *Journal of Public Economics, 88*(9), 2159–2180.

Effective Altruism Forum. (n.d.). *Expected value*. Retrieved January 27, 2024 from https://forum.effectivealtruism.org/topics/expected-value

Fischer, B. (2022, October 31). *An introduction to the Moral Weight Project*. Rethink Priorities. Retrieved January 27, 2024 from https://rethinkpriorities.org/publications/an-introduction-to-the-moral-weight-project

Gates, B. (2021). *How to avoid a climate disaster: The solutions we have and the breakthroughs we need*. Alfred A. Knopf.

Grace, K. (2010, December 20). Estimation is the best we have. *Meteuphoric* (blog). Retrieved January 27, 2024 from https://meteuphoric.com/2010/12/20/estimation-is-the-best-we-have/

Greaves, H. (2017). Population axiology. *Philosophy Compass, 12*(11), Article e12442.

Gregory, A. G., & Howard, D. (2009). The nonprofit starvation cycle. *Stanford Social Innovation Review, 7*(4), 49–53.

Halstead, J. (2018, May). *Climate change cause area report*. Founders Pledge. https://www.founderspledge.com/downloads/fp-climate-change

Halstead, J., Schubert, S., Millum, J., Engelbert, M., Wilkinson, H., & Snowden, J. (2021, January 14). *Effective altruism: An elucidation and a defence*. Centre for Effective Altruism. Retrieved February 1, 2024 from https://www.centreforeffectivealtruism.org/blog/effective-altruism-an-elucidation-and-a-defence

Hamory, J., Miguel, E., Walker, M., Kremer, M., & Baird, S. (2021). Twenty-year economic impacts of deworming. *Proceedings of the National Academy of Sciences of the United States of America, 118*(14), e2023185118. https://doi.org/10.1073/pnas.2023185118

Harsanyi, J. C. (1990). Interpersonal utility comparisons. In J. Eatwell, M. Milgate, & P. Newman (Eds.), *Utility and probability* (pp. 128–133). Palgrave Macmillan. https://doi.org/10.1007/978-1-349-20568-4_17

Hausman, D. (1995). The impossibility of interpersonal utility comparisons. *Mind: A Quarterly Review of Psychology and Philosophy, 104*(415), 473–490.

High Impact Athletes. (2022, January). *Charity. Where results matter more than ever*. https://highimpactathletes.org/impact. Retrieved January 15, 2024.

Hirose, I. (2014). *Egalitarianism*. Routledge.

Hsieh, N.-h., & Andersson, H. (2021, July 14). Incommensurable values. In E. N. Zalta (Ed.), *Stanford encyclopedia of philosophy* (fall 2021 ed.). https://plato.stanford.edu/entries/value-incommensurable/

Jain, H. K. (2010). *Green revolution: History, impact and future*. Studium Press.

Karnofsky, H. (2016, April 4). *Hits-based giving*. Open Philanthropy. Retrieved January 27, 2024 from https://www.openphilanthropy.org/research/hits-based-giving/

Kassirer, S., & Touré-Tillery, M. T.-T. (2023). *Donating time or money: Which altruism feels more effective?* [Unpublished manuscript]. Kellogg School of Management, Northwestern University.

Layard, R., & Oparina, E. (2021). Living long and living well: The WELLBY approach. In J. F. Helliwell, R. Layard, J. D. Sachs, J. E. de Neve, L. B. Aknin, & S. Wang (Eds.), *World happiness report* (pp. 191–208). Sustainable Development Solutions Network.

MacAskill, W., Bykvist, K., & Ord, T. (2020). *Moral uncertainty*. Oxford University Press.

Miguel, E., & Kremer, M. (2004). Worms: Identifying impacts on education and health in the presence of treatment externalities. *Econometrica: Journal of the Econometric Society*, 72(1), 159–217.

Muehlhauser, L. (2018, January). *2017 Report on consciousness and moral patienthood*. Open Philanthropy. Retrieved January 27, 2024 from https://www.openphilanthropy.org/research/2017-report-on-consciousness-and-moral-patienthood/

Narveson, J. (1973). Moral problems of population. *The Monist*, 57(1), 62–86.

Pallotta, D. (2013). *The way we think about charity is dead wrong* [Video]. TED Conferences. https://www.ted.com/talks/dan_pallotta_the_way_we_think_about_charity_is_dead_wrong?language=en

QGiv. (n.d.). *The overhead myth: What's all the fuss about?* Retrieved January 27, 2024, from https://www.qgiv.com/blog/the-overhead-myth/

Rabinowicz, W. (2009). Broome and the intuition of neutrality. *Philosophical Issues: A Supplement to Nous*, 19, 389–411.

Richardson, H. S. (1994). *Practical reasoning about final ends*. Cambridge University Press.

Sebo, J. (2022). *Saving animals, saving ourselves: Why animals matter for pandemics, climate change, and other catastrophes*. Oxford University Press.

Sinnott-Armstrong, W. (1985). Moral dilemmas and incomparability. *American Philosophical Quarterly*, 22(4), 321–329.

Steele, K. & Stéfansson, H. O. (2020, October 9). Decision Theory. In E. N. Zalta (Ed.), *Stanford encyclopedia of philosophy* (winter 2020 ed.). https://plato.stanford.edu/entries/decision-theory/

The Life You Can Save. (n.d.). *Support The Life You Can Save*. Retrieved January 27, 2024 from https://www.thelifeyoucansave.org/invest/

Todd, B. (2020, December). *Where's the best place to volunteer?* 80,000 Hours. https://80000hours.org/articles/volunteering/.Retrieved January 15, 2024.

Todd, B. (2021, September). *Counterfactuals and how they change our view of what does good*. 80,000 Hours. Retrieved January 27, 2024 from https://80000hours.org/articles/counterfactuals/

Townsend, M., & Hoeijmakers, S. (2023, March 31). *2020–2022 Impact evaluation*. Giving What We Can. Retrieved January 27, 2024 from https://www.givingwhatwecan.org/en-US/impact

Wing, K., Hager, M. A., Rooney, P. M., & Pollak, T. (2004). *Lessons for boards from the nonprofit overhead cost project*. Urban Institute and Indiana University. https://www.urban.org/sites/default/files/publication/58171/411119-Lessons-for-Boards-from-the-Nonprofit-Overhead-Cost-Project.PDF

Zeckhauser, R., & Shepard, D. (1976). Where now for saving lives? *Law and Contemporary Problems*, 40(4), 5–45.

PART II
INTERVENTIONS

6
Information, Nudges, and Incentives

To overcome the psychological obstacles to effective altruism, we can employ a range of strategies which differ in terms of both ambition and tractability. We will look at the full range of such strategies in Part II.

In this chapter, we look at a relatively modest strategy, which works with people's values and preferences, instead of trying to change them. We explore techniques that can help people to be more effective without fundamentally changing their values. In Chapter 7, in turn, we study whether we can identify people who are especially positively inclined toward effective altruism. If so, outreach efforts could target those people since they could be more receptive to the effective altruist message. And in Chapter 8, we look at the most ambitious strategy: spreading values conducive to helping others effectively. This strategy would make a big difference if it succeeded but is hard to implement. Finally, in Chapter 9, we discuss what individuals who are persuaded of effective altruism could do to maximize their own impact.

But let's turn to the more modest techniques that are the focus of this chapter. We will cover three types of such techniques: provision of information, nudging, and incentives. These techniques have primarily been tested in the context of charitable giving, and we will therefore mostly focus on donation decisions. However, we believe that modest techniques could also be applied to other altruistic efforts, such as volunteering and career choice.

Providing Information

As we saw in Part I, people have many misconceptions about how to help others effectively, and these misconceptions are major obstacles to effective altruism. Can we dispel them, and if so, does that make people's help more effective?

Our short answer is yes: It can help. Granted, providing people with more accurate information will not make everyone help in the most effective way. Incorrect beliefs are not the only type of obstacle to effective altruism.

Effective Altruism and the Human Mind. Stefan Schubert and Lucius Caviola, Oxford University Press.
© Oxford University Press 2024. DOI: 10.1093/oso/9780197757376.003.0007

People also have preferences that conflict with effectiveness, and provision of factual information normally doesn't affect them. But in general, we can make people help more effectively by providing information about relevant facts: what effectiveness is, how effectiveness relates to overhead costs, the pros and cons of splitting your donations, and so on.

An obvious but important reason people don't help effectively is that they are simply unaware of the most effective ways of helping. As we saw in Chapter 1, almost no one knows about the most effective charities (Caviola et al., 2020). Would people be more inclined to donate to these highly effective charities if they were informed about them?

To find out, the two of us and Jason Nemirow ran two studies where we divided the participants into a control condition and an experimental condition (Caviola et al., 2020). Participants in the control condition were asked, "Suppose we gave you $1000 to donate to any charity. You are free to choose any charity out of all real charities in the world. Which charity would you donate to?" We found that, across the two studies, not a single of the 167 participants picked a charity that experts classify as being among the most effective charities in the world (see also Chapter 1).

In the experimental condition, we let participants read a short paragraph explaining the concept of charity effectiveness and the fact that some charities are much more effective than others. We also told them about the charity evaluator GiveWell and added a link to GiveWell's website that lists some of the world's most effective charities. However, participants were free to ignore this information, and we didn't force them to go to the website. Nevertheless, when we asked these participants where they would donate, we found that this information made a major difference. Whereas no one chose one of the most effective charities in the control condition, 41% (84/207) of the participants who had been thus informed did. This suggests that surprisingly many people would want to give to effective charities if they only knew about them.

There are some studies that didn't find any effects of effectiveness information, which thus might seem to contradict our results at first glance. Dean Karlan and Daniel Wood (2017) found that scientific impact information didn't increase donations (except among large donors) in a direct mail fundraising experiment; and Robin Bergh and David Reinstein (2021) have made similar findings. However, these studies try to answer a slightly different question, namely whether effectiveness information increases total donations. We rather ask whether effectiveness information can steer donations that would have occurred anyway toward more effective charities. That seems intuitively much more likely, especially since donors explicitly say that they find effectiveness an important criterion in charity choice (Chapter 1; Hope Consulting, 2010).

In another set of studies, we looked at whether the overhead myth can be debunked and whether that would make people donate more effectively. Remember the studies from Chapter 5, where we found that participants on average would choose a charity with low overhead costs and a medium level of cost-effectiveness over a charity with high overhead costs and a high level of cost-effectiveness. In other words, overhead took precedence over cost-effectiveness, even though cost-effectiveness is what really matters from the point of view of the beneficiaries of our donations. But the misconception of the relationship between overhead and cost-effectiveness can be debunked, as we saw in Chapter 5. Here is an excerpt of our explanation of the concepts of overhead and cost-effectiveness (Caviola et al., 2020, Supplementary Materials to Study 1a, p. 7).

> Many people believe charities should have low overhead costs because they think that overhead costs are wasted money and therefore lower effectiveness. However, research has shown that high overhead costs do not predict low cost-effectiveness. . . . [O]verhead costs are usually required to make the charities effective. For example, charities need to hire competent staff and build infrastructure critical to accomplishing their mission. High overhead costs do not mean that the charity is wasting money. The only relevant indicator of how effective a charity is, is cost-effectiveness.

As we saw in Chapter 5, this information made a substantial difference, making the average participant switch from the low-overhead charity to the more effective high-overhead charity. In other words, many participants accepted our debunking information and chose the more effective charity, indicating that we can dispel the overhead myth by providing better information about the relationship between overhead and effectiveness.

Other research has also found that it's possible to mitigate overhead aversion by explaining why overhead is necessary. Elizabeth Keenan and Ayelet Gneezy (2016, p. 130) gave participants in a study of theirs the following explanation:

Most donors prefer for their donations to be used directly on programming costs. What these individuals do not understand, however, is that in order for a charity to successfully fulfill its mission it must also incur administrative and fundraising costs, making donations spent on overhead also meaningful and significant.

This explanation increased participants' tendency to support overhead (relative to a control condition where no such explanation was provided), giving further support to the notion that debunking misconceptions about overhead can change donor behavior.

But the overhead myth isn't the only misconception that we can debunk by providing accurate information. We have also found that people are more likely to donate to charities addressing ongoing health issues in the developing world instead of charities addressing more urgent disasters when informed that the former are more effective (see Chapter 1; Caviola et al., 2020). Similarly, we have found that people are more likely to donate to charities targeting distant poor people when informed that they are more effective than local charities (see Chapter 3). And we have found that people are more likely to donate to charities whose interventions involve risk if informed that this would, in expectation, be more effective (see Chapter 5; Caviola et al., 2020). Thus, our research suggests that we can at least to an extent debunk a whole range of misconceptions about charity effectiveness and that doing so can increase the effectiveness of giving.

Real-World Examples

So far, we have looked at the effects of information provision in the lab. But there are also real-world examples of how providing information about charity effectiveness can make people's giving more effective.

A pioneer organization in this domain is the previously mentioned GiveWell (see Chapters 1, 3, and 5). GiveWell analyzes the cost-effectiveness of charities focused on global poverty and health and recommends a small number of the most effective of these charities to donors. It was not the first organization to rate or recommend charities, but when it was founded in 2007, it was unusual in its systematic focus on effectiveness in the sense used in this book (Chapter 5). GiveWell's founders Holden Karnofsky and Elie Hassenfeld both worked at a hedge fund prior to launching GiveWell.

They had planned to give away part of their earnings to charity and wanted to find out what charities are most effective. At the time, there wasn't a lot of information about charity effectiveness, so they took matters into their own hands. They studied the relative effectiveness of different charities themselves and eventually ended up launching GiveWell (Pitney, 2015). GiveWell (2023) raised more than $600 million for effective charities during 2022.

In recent years, several similar charity evaluators have been established. Some are focused on a particular cause. For instance, Animal Charity Evaluators focuses on researching and recommending effective charities that promote animal welfare. There are also charity evaluators that focus on particular groups of donors—such as Founders Pledge, which recommends charities to start-up founders who want to give away part of their personal proceeds when they sell their businesses.

Of course, these recommendations will only work insofar as people trust the rating organizations and are willing to defer to them. Many people prefer to decide for themselves and are reluctant to trust ratings. Whether that attitude is warranted or not depends on the quality of the rating organization, but in general, it seems that people are overly inclined to trust their own judgments over recommendations from researchers on charity effectiveness. It is true that we shouldn't trust experts blindly, but we should at least give people who have done extensive research a fair hearing. As we will see in in the next chapter (Chapter 7), to help others effectively, we need to be epistemically humble and willing to listen to people whose knowledge is greater than our own. But, unfortunately, we don't always do that, and that is probably another part of why most donations aren't going to the most effective charities.

Thus, it's important to emphasize again that merely providing information will not make everyone's help perfectly effective. Other obstacles stand in the way of effective altruism besides a lack of accurate information. But still, our reading of the evidence is that, in many contexts, providing accurate information about effectiveness can make a real difference.

One advantage of charity recommendations is that they allow donors to be effective even if they are not particularly knowledgeable themselves. People often have many misconceptions, each of which can block them from donating to one the most effective charities. For instance, a failure to give to an effective charity that has high overhead, addresses a recurrent problem, and helps distant beneficiaries may be overdetermined by misconceptions about overhead, recurrent versus urgent problems, and local versus distant causes, respectively. In such cases, dispelling just one misconception isn't sufficient. You need to dispel all of them since a single remaining misconception may stop people from giving to the effective charity in question. Needless to say, that can be hard. This means that it can be very valuable to directly recommend specific charities. That may allow us to circumvent all the misconceptions in one go.

Moreover, it is often unrealistic to expect people to proactively do their own rigorous research to identify the most effective charities. Most people have neither the time, the desire, nor the ability to become charity experts themselves. Relying on expert recommendations therefore seems like an effective solution. People regularly make use of expert recommendations for consumer goods and services (cars, hotels, trips, etc.), and it's natural to extend that model to charities.

Expert recommendations can also be useful when it comes to other forms of do-gooding. Maybe the best example within effective altruism is career advice, which has been pioneered by the organization 80,000 Hours. (The name *80,000 Hours* is based on the rough number of hours people typically work in their careers.) 80,000 Hours gives career advice to young people who want to have an impact through their careers. Just as most donors don't know what charities are most effective, most young people looking to have an impact don't know what careers are most effective. And just as the differences in impact between charities are large, the differences in impact between different careers are also large (Todd, 2023). Therefore, we need not only charity recommenders like GiveWell but also career advice organizations like 80,000 Hours. When giving advice, 80,000 Hours looks both at how generally impactful a career or job might be and at the advisee's personal talents and dispositions.

Nudging

Another modest strategy for behavior change is *nudging*, which seeks to alter people's behavior by changing the "choice architecture"—that is, the context in which a choice is made—without changing their preferences. Nudging was made famous by Richard Thaler and Cass Sunstein in their book *Nudge* (2008) and has received an enormous amount of attention. For instance, government agencies—such as the British government's "Nudge Unit" (The Behavioural Insights Team) and similar units in other countries—have used it for everything from fine payment compliance to retirement savings plans (Halpern, 2015; Hiscox et al., 2018; Thaler & Sunstein, 2008).

But nudging can also be used in the context of charitable giving and other sorts of altruistic endeavors (Everett et al., 2015). By changing the choice architecture, we can nudge people to donate to more effective charities, even though they retain preferences that normally tend to conflict with effectiveness—such as preferences for specific charities and preferences for splitting donations across multiple charities. Indeed, we can turn some of these preferences into a tool for making giving more effective. Let us look at a concrete example of this.

Donation Bundling

As we saw in Chapter 4, many people like to split their donations across multiple charities (Caviola et al., 2020; Sharps & Schroeder, 2019). This preference for splitting often leads to less effective giving since it is usually more effective to concentrate our donations toward the most effective charity. But by changing the choice architecture, we can actually use this preference to increase the effectiveness of people's giving.

By default, most people don't donate anything to the most effective charities. But since they like splitting, they may be open to splitting their donations between the charity they already support (which tends to be less effective) and a highly effective charity. That way, the effectiveness of their donations may be increased.

Lucius Caviola and Joshua Greene (2023) tested this idea in a study with 1039 US participants, divided into control and experimental conditions. The participants were first asked what their "favorite charity" is; that is, what charity they care most about out of all the charities in the world. Subsequently, they were presented with Evidence Action's Deworm the World Initiative, a highly effective charity program consisting of the distribution of pills against parasitic worms in developing countries in Africa. Deworm the World Initiative is remarkably effective at alleviating suffering and promoting health, largely thanks to the very cheap pills it distributes. Participants were informed about Deworm the World Initiative's work and told that it is one of the most effective charities in the world.

They were then asked whether they preferred giving to their favorite charity or to Deworm the World Initiative and (in a second step) how much they wanted to donate and how much they wanted to save for themselves provided they had $100. Control condition participants were required to allocate any donations they chose to make toward one charity; that is, they were not allowed to split their donations across the two charities. Unsurprisingly, most of these participants (82%) chose to donate to their favorite charity, whereas only 18% chose to donate to the highly effective Deworm the World Initiative. While the mere information that Deworm the World Initiative is highly effective thus led some people to prioritize it, they were a minority. Most control condition participants preferred to donate to their favorite charity, even after learning about Deworm the World Initiative's effectiveness.

Participants in the experimental condition were faced with almost the same setup, except they were also given the option to split any donations of theirs evenly between their favorite charity and Deworm the World Initiative. We refer to this as a *bundle* option as it bundles a donation to the participants' favorite charity with a donation to a highly effective charity (Milkman et al., 2012). As expected, this bundle option was very popular, chosen by 51% of participants (of the remaining 49%, 46% gave the whole amount to their favorite charity and 3% gave the whole amount to Deworm the World Initiative). Due to the popularity of the bundle option, total donations to the effective charity increased by 76% relative to the control condition. Thus, simply giving people the option to split their donations between their favorite charity and a highly effective charity had a big effect on the effectiveness of their giving.

The bundling technique draws on several of the insights about psychological obstacles to effective altruism that we covered in Part I. As we saw in Chapter 1, people tend to have favorite charities they prefer to give to even after they've been informed that other charities are more effective. At the same time, they also have a preference for effectiveness: Everything else being equal, they prefer more effective charities. Thus, they have two preferences that conflict whenever the most effective charities aren't the same as the charities they personally care most about (i.e., most of the time). Usually, their preference for particular charities is stronger and trumps their preference for effectiveness. That is why most people continue to give to charities that are emotionally appealing even after they've learned that another charity is more effective.

However, the fact that most people have a preference for effectiveness gives us a foot in the door. It means that people can be nudged into giving to more effective charities if we create the right choice architecture. Giving people the option to split (and making that option salient) is such a nudge. Again, people tend to like splitting their donations. They find splitting fair and are uncomfortable with entirely deprioritizing a charity.

Relatedly, people may also experience diminishing marginal utility from giving more to the same charity (Chapter 4). While they like giving to their favorite charity, their subjective utility may not scale with the amount they give to that charity. They might feel more strongly about the first $50 they give to their favorite charity than about the next $50. This means that even though most people give their first dollar to their favorite charity, priorities may shift as their donations increase. As the marginal utility that they derive from additional dollars to their favorite charity progressively decreases, it may at some point drop below the utility that they derive from giving a dollar to the effective charity. This may explain why many participants split their donations between their favorite charity and the highly effective Deworm the World Initiative.

A study that Caviola and Greene (2023) conducted illuminates these diminishing marginal returns. They presented 299 US participants with two options: to give the full amount to their favorite charity or to choose a *favorite-effective bundle*—to split their donations between their favorite charity and the effective Deworm the World Initiative. Caviola and Greene gave the participants multiple donation tasks and varied the splitting rates in the bundle option. In the first task, the bundle option involved giving 10% of the donation to the favorite charity and 90% to the effective charity (a *10/90 bundle*); in the second, the proportion was 40/60; in the third, it was 60/40; and in the fourth, it was 90/10. As expected, participants were more likely to choose the bundle the greater the share that was allocated toward their favorite charity. But notably, their preference for the bundle did not scale linearly. Only 31% of participants chose a 10/90 bundle, whereas 46% chose a 40/60 bundle: a 15% difference. By contrast, there was only a 5% difference between the 60/40 and 90/10 bundles (59% vs. 64%). The difference between these two differences (15% vs. 5%) was significant. That means that among bundles where only a small share of donations is allocated to the participants' favorite charity, participants are quite sensitive to increases in that share; but among bundles where that share is already large, they are much less sensitive to further increases. This may be best explained by diminishing marginal utility of additional money toward the favorite charity. Most people find it important that a sizable part of their donation is allocated to their favorite charity, but once they've donated a decent amount to that charity, they are willing to give the rest to a highly effective charity. (However, a minority of donors are insistent on giving exclusively to their favorite charity, meaning they reject all bundle options no matter what the proportions are.)

In our view, the bundling technique that we have presented works partly because it allows people to satisfy both their preference for effectiveness and their preference for their favorite charity. But there is a rival hypothesis, namely that people's preference for splitting their donations in itself suffices to explain why bundling works. According to this hypothesis, people have a general preference for bundles of charities, whatever their qualities. To test that hypothesis, Caviola and Greene (2023) set up a study where they presented 227 participants with three different 50/50 bundles. All three bundles involved their favorite charity and another charity: one which was said to be highly effective, one which was said to be highly popular, and one which lacked description. Caviola and Greene found that whereas 56% of participants chose the bundle involving an effective charity, only 21% chose the bundle involving a popular charity and 22% the bundle involving a charity without a description. This suggests that most people have a particular preference for favorite-effective bundles, contradicting the rival hypothesis. Unlike the other bundles, favorite-effective bundles can satisfy both their preference to give to a charity they personally care about and their preference to give effectively.

Notably, choosing a favorite-effective bundle can also have reputational benefits. In another study, Caviola and Greene (2023) asked participants to rate the perceived warmth and competence of other donors. (Research on judgments of character often focuses on perceived warmth and perceived competence [Fiske et al, 2002].) They were interested in whether donors who choose a 50/50 favorite-effective bundle would be judged differently from donors who exclusively give to their favorite charity and donors who exclusively give to an effective charity. As might be expected, they found that donors who chose their favorite charity were seen as warmer than those who chose an effective charity, whereas the reverse was true for judgments of competence. Donors who chose the bundle got the best of both worlds, however: They were seen as more competent (but not less warm) than donors who prioritized their favorite charity and warmer (but not less competent) than donors who prioritized the effective charity (Caviola & Greene, 2023). Thus, by giving both to their favorite charity and to a highly effective charity, donors signal both warmth and competence.

The bundling technique is a surprisingly useful tool for making giving more effective. But how can we make people consider making bundled donations? In principle, people could already split their donations between their favorite charity and a highly effective charity. But most people don't do that, in part because they don't even consider that option. Let's look at how we can use another technique to address that issue by raising the salience of the possibility of bundling donations.

Incentivizing Effectiveness Through Donation Matching

The technique we have in mind is *donation matching*: matching any donations made with additional dollars. As we will see, donation matching also directly incentivizes people to give more to effective charities, relative to what the bundling technique can achieve by itself. Thus, it can increase donations to effective charities in two ways: indirectly, via making the bundling option salient, and more directly, by providing incentives to prioritize effective charities.

Fundraisers often offer matches to increase donations. They promise to top up each dollar given to a particular charity with, for example, another dollar (or 50 cents or $2, etc.). In some cases, this has proven an effective strategy to increase donations (Karlan & List, 2007). For instance, Uri Gneezy, Elizabeth Keenan, and Ayelet Gneezy (2014) have shown that this strategy can be used to mitigate overhead aversion since people give more to charity if a matching donor promises to cover the overhead. Drawing on these insights, Caviola and Greene (2023) developed a new matching technique that can be used specifically to encourage more effective giving.

Conjoining matching with bundling, this technique offers increasing matching rates for favorite-effective bundles in proportion to the fraction of the donation allocated to the effective charity. In yet another study, Caviola and Greene (2023) presented 421 participants with the same three donation options we encountered before: to give exclusively to their favorite charity, to give exclusively to a highly effective charity, or to split their donation 50/50 between the two charities. But this time, they informed participants that their donations would be matched at rates that depended on what option they chose. The more money they allocated to the effective charity, the greater the match percentage would be. If they gave the full amount to their favorite charity, the match was only 5%, whereas it was 25% for the 50/50 split option, and 50% for donations fully concentrated toward the effective charity. As previously, participants could allocate up to $100 (and they could also keep all or part of this sum for themselves).

These matches had a big effect relative to a control condition, where no matches were offered. On average, participants in the experimental condition gave $27.47 to the effective charity, $9.70 (55%) more than participants in the control condition (Caviola & Greene, 2023). Thus, by offering particularly large matches to donations to effective charities, we can increase donations to them relative to what the bundling technique can achieve by itself. And again, the matching technique can also be used to advertise the bundling technique. In the real world, donors would normally not pay attention to the bundling option unless they were provided some tangible reason to do so. But the presence of matching offers gives them such a tangible reason, and thus makes the possibility of bundling their donations much more salient. We will return to how this strategy can be implemented in the real world in the next section.

One reason the matching technique is so effective is that people are presented with the three options side by side—in joint evaluation (as opposed to separate evaluation, where different options are not directly compared). As we saw in Chapters 2, 4, and 5, joint evaluation allows for straightforward comparisons between options and makes it salient if there are any differences between them. In this case, it is very salient that one gets larger matches for options that allocate more funds to the effective charity than for options that allocate more funds to one's favorite charity. In fact, the matching rates don't even have to be very high to have a substantial effect on donation choices. The mere fact that donors are getting a larger match if they prioritize the effective charity goes a long way, even if the absolute amounts added as donation matches aren't very large (Caviola & Greene, 2023).

Giving Multiplier

These studies show that bundling combined with the kind of increasing-rates matching we just described work in the laboratory. But do these techniques work in the real world? To test that, Caviola and Greene launched a new donation platform called Giving Multiplier with the help of Fabio Kuhn and Daniel Rütheman (https://givingmultiplier.org/). The aim of Giving Multiplier is to encourage donations to effective charities and to introduce new donors to the concept of effective giving. As we will see, it makes use of both the bundling and the matching techniques. In short, it gives donors the opportunity to split their donations between their favorite charity and an effective charity and provides matches that specifically encourage more effective giving.

Users who land on the website are first asked to select their favorite charity, which can be any charity recognized in the United States (though Giving Multiplier is also open for users outside of the United States). They are then presented with a short list of highly effective charities chosen by experts from the effective altruism community. In January 2024, the recommended charities were as follows:

- Against Malaria Foundation (distributes antimalarial bed nets in developing countries)
- Evidence Action's Deworm the World Initiative (distributes deworming pills to children to combat worm infection)
- Give Directly (provides direct cash transfers to households in developing countries)
- Helen Keller International (prevents poor vision and other poor health outcomes in developing countries)
- New Incentives (provides cash transfers to incentivize immunization in developing countries)
- The Good Food Institute (develops and promotes alternatives to animal products, such as plant-based meat substitutes)
- The Humane League (promotes animal welfare via multiple strategies, including corporate campaigns and advertising for plant-based food)
- Clean Air Task Force (works to reduce climate pollutants through research, advocacy, and related strategies)
- Johns Hopkins Center for Health Security (works to mitigate epidemics and related disasters through advancing policy, science, and technology)

Donors are asked to choose one of these charities as their preferred effective charity. After they've chosen a favorite charity and an effective charity, they are asked how much they would like to donate in total.

Subsequently, donors are presented with a slider to determine what proportions of their donation they want to allocate toward their favorite charity and their chosen effective charity, respectively. They can choose to give between 10% and 100% to the effective charity (in 10% steps), with the remainder going to their favorite charity. The more they give to the effective charity, the more their donation will be topped up by matching funds. For instance, if they give their full donation to their chosen effective charity, they will receive an 80% match (i.e., a $100 donation will be topped up by $80), whereas if they give 90% to their favorite charity and 10% to the effective charity, they will receive an 8% match. (These match percentages are from 2024 and may be subject to change.)

Giving Multiplier has quickly built a user base since it was launched in November 2020. Word of Giving Multiplier was primarily spread via unpaid media coverage such as articles in the *Los Angeles Times*, Project Syndicate, MarketWatch, and Vox.com, as well as podcast appearances on Waking Up (Sam Harris), Happiness Lab (Laurie Santos), and Mindscape (Sean Carroll; Albrecht, 2021; Carroll, 2021; Caviola & Greene, 2020; Harris, 2020; Samuel, 2020; Santos, 2022; Singer & Caviola, 2020). The Giving Multiplier team also introduced a recruit-a-friend system that allowed donors (including all Giving What We Can members) to invite their friends and family members to try effective giving through Giving Multiplier (Freeman, 2023).

After 3 years (in January 2024), Giving Multiplier has fundraised a total of $3 million from nearly 8000 donations (Giving Multiplier, 2024). Over $1.8 million has been allocated to the recommended effective charities, and of those, it is estimated (based on donor surveys) that nearly $1.6m would not have been donated to effective charities if it weren't for Giving Multiplier. The donations have come from approximately 3400 donors, most of whom are new to effective altruism. Moreover, most of the donors have indicated that they didn't know about the effective charity they chose to support before reading about it on GivingMultiplier.org. Hundreds of donors have sent positive messages, and the overall reception has been very positive. In 2021, the Giving Multiplier team received an award from IDEO (in partnership with the Bill & Melinda Gates Foundation and Better Giving Studio) for having created an innovative concept in the digital giving space (https://www.bettergivingstudio.com/announcing-finalists-of-the-reimagine-charitable-giving-challenge/).

Donor Coordination Through Micro-Matching

By January 2024, donations via Giving Multiplier had used nearly $1m in matching funds. Where do these matching funds come from? You might think they come from some major effective altruist-aligned philanthropist who wants to encourage effective giving. That would indeed have been a plausible strategy. But, in fact, Giving Multiplier uses a quite different approach to ensure the provision of sufficient matching funding. We call this technique *micro-matching* since it relies on matches from small donors. Essentially, it is a form of coordination between donors, which allows them to satisfy their preferences better.

Donors have a wide variety of preferences. Some are primarily interested in allocating money to their favorite charity and only put a moderate weight on effectiveness. Others find effectiveness very important. And still others are in-between.

These individual differences mean that donor coordination can be useful. People who care strongly about effectiveness would, by default, direct most or all of their donations directly to a highly effective charity. But there is another and more indirect way for them to have an even bigger impact. Instead of directly donating to effective charities, they could provide matching funds to other donors, thereby incentivizing them to donate more to highly effective charities than they otherwise would have done. In other words, they could become micro-matchers.

The matching study described earlier provides empirical evidence that micro-matching can be an effective strategy to raise funds for high-impact charities. Remember that in that study matching increased donations to the effective charity by $9.70 per donor (Caviola & Greene, 2023). But notably, these matched donations only consumed $3.73 per donor in matching funds. In other words, each matching dollar led to approximately $2.60 in additional donations to the effective charity. That suggests that a donor who wants to maximize donations to effective charities could have a greater impact by donating to the Giving Multiplier matching system instead of donating directly to one of the effective charities. If a sufficient number of donors would be willing to provide some micro-matching funds, the whole donation system could become entirely financially self-sustaining. Donors who are inclined to split their donations across the two charities could take advantage of the matching funds provided by donors focused on effectiveness. Everybody would be able to satisfy their respective preferences without any need for outside funding.

Caviola, Greene, and the rest of the team applied this technique on the Giving Multiplier platform. They explained to donors why they could have a greater (albeit more indirect) impact by providing matching funds than by donating directly to one of the effective charities. They then allowed them to choose between donating directly to their chosen charities and becoming micro-matchers.

This worked surprisingly well. No less than 38% of Giving Multiplier donors let part or all of their donations go into the matching system, and that sufficed to make it entirely self-sustaining. That is, there was no need for external funding to cover the required matching costs. This has held true since the launch of the website, and it seems plausible that there won't be any need for external funding in the future either, even if the website scales.

The Giving Multiplier matching system obviously shares some features with other matching systems, but it also differs from most of them in important ways. The typical matching campaign involves a philanthropist or an organization providing a certain amount of funds that match donations that other donors allocate toward a specific charity. Depending on the context, that means it's possible that the matching funder would have donated the same amount to the charity even if smaller donors wouldn't have used up all the announced matching funds. In such cases, there is no true matching, some argue, since the smaller donations looking to get matched don't actually increase the amount of matching funds going to the charity in question (Karnofsky, 2016). There is no counterfactual impact associated with the donation matches (see Chapter 5).

But the Giving Multiplier matching system is different. In contrast to such matching systems, the Giving Multiplier matching system allows donors to have a counterfactual matching impact in two different ways. First, donors can influence which specific charities receive matching funds. Giving Multiplier uses nine effective charities and allows donors to pick any charity recognized in the United States as their favorite charity. That means that if a particular donor decides not to take advantage of the matching funds but leaves them for another donor, it's unlikely that the matching funds would be allocated toward the same charities. Instead, it's likely that the other donor would choose other charities, which would benefit from the matching funds.

Second, donors can have a counterfactual impact by encouraging other visitors to the site to provide more matching funds, which in turn can encourage further counterfactual donations in a supply-demand cycle. Unlike in ordinary matching campaigns, the amount of matching funds isn't fixed but is likely to increase if the demand for matching funds increases. In this way, donors can counterfactually affect the decisions of matching funders. The matching system is explained in great detail on the Giving Multiplier website to ensure that donors understand how it works (Giving Multiplier, n.d.). Donors must also explicitly indicate that they've understood where the matching funds come from before they donate.

Conclusion

There are many ways to make people's help more effective without changing their fundamental values. In this chapter, we have looked at several techniques, such as providing information, nudging, and giving incentives that encourage more effective donations. Several strategies have been shown to work in the real world, such as GiveWell-style charity recommendations, donation bundling, and matching. There are, no doubt, many other strategies that could be tried and that should be researched.

These strategies are easy to test and often increase real-world donations. As we have seen, Giving Multiplier has already directed millions of dollars to effective charities. And charity recommendations can clearly make a big difference.

But a disadvantage of these interventions is that they may not, in and of themselves, lead to the radical change of the world of do-gooding we ideally want. The large differences in effectiveness between different ways of helping mean that it is especially valuable if someone wholeheartedly engages with effective altruism. That way, they may be willing to challenge themselves to choose the very most effective strategies, which people with a less strong enthusiasm for effective altruism might not do. In the next two chapters, we will look at how we could find people who are inclined toward such wholehearted enthusiasm for effective altruism and how effective altruism can be spread more widely.

References

Albrecht, L. (2021, December 23). *Torn between donating to a charity you care about vs. one that will do the most good? Try this "Giving Multiplier."* Market Watch. https://www.marketwatch.com/story/for-giving-tuesday-a-tool-helps-you-give-to-the-most-effective-charities-without-criticizing-your-values-11638282037

Bergh, R., & Reinstein, D. (2021). Empathic and numerate giving: The joint effects of victim images and charity evaluations. *Social Psychological and Personality Science*, *12*(3), 407–416.

Carroll, S. (2021, December 6). *Joshua Greene on morality, psychology, and trolley problems* [Audio podcast]. Sean Carroll's Mindscape. https://www.preposterousuniverse.com/podcast/2021/12/06/176-joshua-greene-on-morality-psychology-and-trolley-problems/

Caviola, L., & Greene, J. (2020, December 17). How to be an effective altruist when giving to charities. *Los Angeles Times*. https://www.latimes.com/opinion/story/2020-12-17/effective-altruism-charity-psychology-morality-donation

Caviola, L., & Greene, J. D. (2023). Boosting the impact of charitable giving with donation bundling and micromatching. *Science Advances, 9*(3), Article ade7987. https://doi.org/10.1126/sciadv.ade7987

Caviola, L., Schubert, S., & Nemirow, J. (2020). The many obstacles to effective giving. *Judgment and Decision Making, 15*(2), 159–172. Supplementary materials at https://osf.io/42ke3/.

Everett, J. A. C., Caviola, L., Kahane, G., Savulescu, J., & Faber, N. S. (2015). Doing good by doing nothing? The role of social norms in explaining default effects in altruistic contexts. *European Journal of Social Psychology, 45*(2), 230–241.

Fiske, S. T., Cuddy, A. J. C., Glick, P., & Xu, J. (2002). A model of (often mixed) stereotype content: Competence and warmth respectively follow from perceived status and competition. *Journal of Personality and Social Psychology, 82*(6), 878–902.

Freeman, L. (2023, August 12). *Giving Multiplier interview with Joshua Greene* [Audio podcast]. Giving What We Can. https://www.givingwhatwecan.org/blog/giving-multiplier-interview-with-joshua-greene

GiveWell. (2023, December). *GiveWell's impact*. https://www.givewell.org/about/impact. Retrieved January 15, 2024.

Giving Multiplier. (2024). *The impact of Giving Multiplier in numbers*. Retrieved January 15, 2024, from https://givingmultiplier.org/impact

Giving Multiplier. (n.d.). *Transparency in donation matching: How does Giving Multiplier work?* Retrieved January 27, 2024, from https://givingmultiplier.org/transparency

Gneezy, U., Keenan, E. A., & Gneezy, A. (2014). Avoiding overhead aversion in charity. *Science, 346*(6209), 632–635.

Halpern, D. (2015). *Inside the nudge unit: How small changes can make a big difference*. Random House.

Harris, S. (2020, December 2). *Doing good; how to be a moral hero* [Audio podcast]. Waking Up. https://dynamic.wakingup.com/pack/PK7W71C

Hiscox, M. J., Copley, S., Brewer, J., Turenko, A., & Wilson, J. (2018). *Effective use of SMS to encourage timely reporting behaviour using digital channels*. Behavioural Economics Team of the Australian Government. https://behaviouraleconomics.pmc.gov.au/projects/effective-use-sms-encourage-timely-reporting-behaviour-using-digital-channels

Hope Consulting. (2010, May). *Money for good: The US market for impact investments and charitable gifts from individual donors and investors*. https://search.issuelab.org/resource/money-for-good-the-us-market-for-impact-investments-and-charitable-gifts-from-individual-donors-and-investors.html

Karlan, D., & List, J. A. (2007). Does price matter in charitable giving? Evidence from a large-scale natural field experiment. *The American Economic Review, 97*(5), 1774–1793.

Karlan, D., & Wood, D. (2017). The effect of effectiveness: Donor response to aid effectiveness in a direct mail fundraising experiment. *Journal of Behavioral and Experimental Economics, 66*, 1–8.

Karnofsky, H. (2016, July 25). Why you shouldn't let "donation matching" affect your giving. *The GiveWell Blog.* https://blog.givewell.org/2011/12/15/why-you-shouldnt-let-donation-matching-affect-your-giving/

Keenan, E., & Gneezy, A. (2016). Understanding and overcoming overhead aversion in charity. *Advances in Consumer Research—North America, 44,* 129–130. https://www.acrwebsite.org/volumes/1021642/volumes/v44/

Milkman, K. L., Mazza, M. C., Shu, L. L., Tsay, C.-J., & Bazerman, M. H. (2012). Policy bundling to overcome loss aversion: A method for improving legislative outcomes. *Organizational Behavior and Human Decision Processes, 117*(1), 158–167.

Pitney, N. (2015, March 26). *That time a hedge funder quit his job and then raised $60 million for charity.* HuffPost. https://www.huffingtonpost.co.uk/entry/elie-hassenfeld-givewell_n_6927320

Samuel, S. (2020, December 17). *How to give a meaningful holiday gift this year.* Vox. https://www.vox.com/future-perfect/22177289/best-meaningful-holiday-gift-charity-donations

Santos, L. (2022, November 29). *How to give more effectively* [Audio podcast]. Pushkin: The Happiness Lab With Dr. Laurie Santos. https://www.pushkin.fm/podcasts/the-happiness-lab-with-dr-laurie-santos/how-to-give-more-effectively

Sharps, D. L., & Schroeder, J. (2019). The preference for distributed helping. *Journal of Personality and Social Psychology, 117*(5), 954–977.

Singer, P., & Caviola, L. (2020, December 7). *Giving with the heart and the head.* Project Syndicate. https://www.project-syndicate.org/commentary/maximizing-efficiency-of-charitable-donations-by-peter-singer-and-lucius-caviola-2020-12?barrier=accespaylog

Thaler, R. H., & Sunstein, C. R. (2008). *Nudge: Improving decisions using the architecture of choice.* Yale University Press.

Todd, B. (2023, February). *The best solutions are far more effective than others.* 80,000 Hours. Retrieved January 27, 2024 from https://80000hours.org/articles/solutions/

7
Finding the Enthusiasts

In Part I, we saw that there are formidable psychological obstacles to effective altruism. But at the same time, a growing number of people view themselves as effective altruists. How can we reconcile these different observations?

Part of the answer is that people's inclinations toward effective altruism vary substantially. So far, we've focused on the tendencies of the average person. We've seen that most people find key effective altruist ideas unintuitive. But that doesn't mean that everyone takes that view. There are big individual differences regarding people's dispositions toward effective altruism. If, say, 1000 people are introduced to effective altruism, different people will react very differently. While some will disagree strongly, others will like effective altruism and want to learn more. And there will, of course, be a spectrum between these two extreme ends. Some people may find the ideas somewhat counterintuitive at first but warm up to them after more engagement.

This suggests an interesting strategy. Instead of trying to reach out indiscriminately to the population at large, outreach efforts could specifically be targeted at those who are more open to effective altruism.

Who are these people who find effective altruism appealing? What psychological traits make people more positively inclined toward effective altruism? Is positive inclination toward effective altruism a single psychological factor, or are there several distinct factors? A deeper understanding of the psychology of people who are drawn toward effective altruism is both practically and theoretically relevant.

It is practically relevant because a better understanding of these effective altruism enthusiasts' psychology and demographic features could help us identify these people. In which countries and regions can we find them? What professions do they have? What have they studied, or what do they study? These are all questions that could be highly informative for anyone who wants to spread the ideas of effective altruism.

Research on individual differences regarding inclinations toward effective altruism could also help to estimate the potential size of effective altruism.

Effective Altruism and the Human Mind. Stefan Schubert and Lucius Caviola, Oxford University Press.
© Oxford University Press 2024. DOI: 10.1093/oso/9780197757376.003.0008

How many potential effective altruists are there? Is it a tiny fraction of the population—say 0.1%? Or a much larger part—say 20%? We have come across very different views on this issue among effective altruist community-builders. It seems important to answer it with careful empirical research.

But learning about the different drivers of interest in effective altruism is also of theoretical interest. It would give us a richer understanding of the various psychological obstacles to effective altruism. How are they related to each other? Are people who tend to overcome one obstacle more disposed to overcome other obstacles? Or are the different obstacles more separate? How many psychologically distinct effective altruist factors are there? Better answers to these questions could increase our understanding of effective altruism as well as the nature of human altruism more generally.

Moral Factors

In a project that we conducted together with our colleagues David Althaus and Joshua Lewis we tried to identify the psychological factors that predict whether someone endorses the core moral ideas of effective altruism.

We set out by devising over 100 items (short statements) about the value of helping effectively and other important moral aspects of effective altruism (Caviola, Althaus, et al., 2022). We then conducted a series of surveys where we asked 534 participants from the US general population to what extent they agreed with the items. These surveys aimed to understand the psychological structure of people's moral attitudes toward effective altruism: in other words, how different attitudes relate to each other. We relied on factor analysis, a statistical method that reduces the number of participant response variables into a small number of core psychological factors. We didn't have a particular hypothesis about what factors we would find. Instead, we planned to see what patterns would emerge from the data.

As we shall see, we found two core moral factors, which we call *expansive altruism* and *effectiveness-focus*. People with a high score on the expansive altruism scale are both (1) willing to give away resources to help others and (2) caring about individuals who are distant from them spatially, temporally, and biologically. Though these two features are conceptually distinct, they correlate so strongly that they should be seen as a single factor from a psychological point of view, according to our research. People who are more impartial with respect to the relationship between themselves and others (i.e., who are less selfish) are also more impartial with respect to different groups of others, whether they're close or distant. On the other hand, effectiveness-focus—the inclination to make tough trade-offs and deprioritize less effective ways of helping, even if they are close to your heart—only correlated weakly ($r = .23$) with expansive altruism and should thus be seen as its own factor. This is an important finding. Expansive altruism and effectiveness-focus could have ended up so closely related that they would be part of one and the same factor, just like the two tendencies that make up the expansive altruism construct did. But it just so happens that there are quite a few expansive altruists who are not effectiveness-focused, and vice versa. Therefore, these two factors—which broadly correspond to the "E" and the "A" in EA (a commonly used acronym for effective altruism)—are psychologically distinct. As we will see, this may help us understand why there are relatively few people who immediately find effective altruism wholly convincing upon hearing about it for the first time. The lack of correlation between the E and the A in effective altruism means that only a relatively small number of people are, as it were, above the bar for effective altruism enthusiasm along both dimensions.

Expansive Altruism

The first factor that we identified is what we call *expansive altruism*. This factor captures people's willingness to help others, including distant others, at a personal cost.

Effective altruism involves at least a moderate level of altruism—a willingness to sacrifice some resources for the sake of others. As we will see in Chapter 9, it doesn't entail extreme levels of altruism, but it does involve a certain amount.

There are, of course, many ideologies and moral philosophies that emphasize the importance of altruism. What is distinctive about effective altruism is thus not primarily the altruism per se (or the amount of altruism it asks for) but rather its type of altruism. Effective altruists are altruistic in specific and unusual ways. As we saw in Chapter 3, most people are altruistic specifically toward people close to them—spatially, temporally, and biologically. By contrast, effective altruists are motivated to help distant beneficiaries as well. To use Peter Singer's (1981) term, effective altruists have an expanded moral circle that includes everyone, regardless of where they live, at what point in time they live, and whether they are humans or animals.

In recent years, psychologists have started to investigate the concept of *moral expansiveness*, building on Singer's philosophical work. They have demonstrated that there are large individual differences in how expansive people's moral circles are (Crimston et al., 2016, 2018). While some people exclusively care about those who are close to them, such as their family and friends, other people also care about distant groups. Our research on expansive altruism is inspired by this research but is specifically geared to identify inclinations toward effective altruism.

As stated, when we conducted factor analyses of the data collected in our surveys, we found that the items relating to altruistically giving resources to others and the items relating to impartiality toward distant others loaded on one and the same factor. We thus decided to call that factor *expansive altruism*. Below we list the six theoretically and statistically most important items in this factor: the *expansive altruism scale*. In one of the surveys of the US general population mentioned above, 259 participants were asked how much they agreed with the items on a scale from 1 (strongly disagree) to 4 (neither agree nor disagree) to 7 (strongly agree).

- As long as my and my family's basic material needs are covered, I want to use a significant amount of my resources (e.g., money or time) to improve the world.
- I am willing to make significant sacrifices for people in need that I don't know and will never meet.
- People in wealthy countries should donate a substantial proportion of their income to make the world a better place.
- I would make a career change if it meant that I could improve the lives of people in need.
- We should put a lot of emphasis on the well-being of people who will live thousands of years from now, even relative to the well-being of people who live today.
- From a moral perspective, the suffering of all beings matters roughly the same, no matter what species they belong to.

We calculated the expansive altruism score as the straight average of the responses on the six items and found that these scores exhibited large individual differences. Some people didn't want to give resources to others, whether they're close or distant, whereas others were more than willing to provide help and to do so in an impartial spirit. The expansive altruism scores were normally distributed with a mean of 4.4 (i.e., close to the midpoint).

Next, we wanted to see whether the expansive altruism scale could predict relevant effective altruist outcome measures. To test that, we asked the participants how they would allocate a certain amount of money. They were given three options: They could keep the money for themselves, give it to the charity that is their personal favorite, or give it to a highly effective charity that helps people in the poorest countries in the world. We found that expansive altruism significantly predicted both the amount participants were willing to give to one of the charities ($r = .34$) and the proportion they were willing to give specifically to the effective charity that helps the poorest people in the world ($r = .29$).

We also presented the same participants with a short introductory text on effective altruism and asked them a series of follow-up questions. Participants were asked about their attitudes toward effective altruism, their interest in learning more about it, and their willingness to take effective altruist–inspired actions. We found that expansive altruism significantly predicted responses on all our outcome measures, including positive attitudes toward the introductory text ($r = .32$) and interest in learning more about effective altruism ($r = .47$). Expansive altruists were also more inclined to say that they might behave in line with effective altruism: They were more likely to say that they would consider donating 10% of their income to effective charities ($r = .42$) and more open to changing their career path to have a higher impact ($r = .49$). These results suggest that expansive altruism predicts enthusiasm about effective altruism in a relevant sense.

We also made some observations about demographic correlations (across all of the 534 participants), for example, that politically liberal ($r = .33$), younger ($r = .16$), and female ($r = .12$) participants tended to score higher on the expansive altruism scale. However, some of these demographic correlations were relatively weak, and we want to caution against reading too much into them as more research is needed.

As stated, these studies used a sample from the US general population. However, effective altruists often come from specific groups, such as university students. Therefore, Lucius Caviola, Erin Morrisey, and Joshua Lewis (2022) conducted a similar study with a relatively representative (in terms of age, gender, and study subject) sample of 938 students from New York University. Participants were presented with the expansive altruism scale and responded to a range of other questions about effective altruism. The mean expansive altruism score in the student sample was 4.6, which was similar to the score in the sample of the general population (4.4). Caviola and his colleagues also replicated the findings that expansive altruism scores are correlated with positive attitudes toward the introductory text about effective altruism ($r = .29$) and interest in learning more about effective altruism ($r = .30$). Moreover, they found that expansive altruism was associated with choosing to donate the $20 payment for completing the study to GiveWell instead of receiving a gift card ($r = .11$).

Finally, we gave the expansive altruism scale to a sample of 226 self-identified effective altruists we had recruited through social media (Caviola, Althaus, et al., 2022). We found that this sample had, as expected, a much higher mean expansive altruism score (5.6) than the samples of students and the US general population. Furthermore, we found that effective altruist participants scored higher on the expansive altruism scale the more they self-identified with effective altruism ($r = .37$). These findings provide further validation that the scale measures what it is supposed to measure.

Effectiveness-Focus

Expansive altruism is necessary for effective altruism, but it's not sufficient. Many people who agree that it is important to help distant individuals are not positively disposed toward effective altruism. For instance, many politically liberal people emphasize the importance of helping distant people, but most of them don't support effective altruism. One reason for that is that there is another factor that determines whether or not someone is positively inclined toward effective altruism: what we call *effectiveness-focus*. Effectiveness-focused people believe that when one helps others or otherwise does good in the world, one should choose the option that does the most good with the available amount of resources. A focus on effectiveness implies overcoming various motivational obstacles to effectiveness, such as scope insensitivity (Chapter 2) and aversion to tough trade-offs (Chapter 4). Many expansive altruists are disinclined to overcome these obstacles, reducing their enthusiasm for effective altruism.

As we saw, we identified the effectiveness-focus factor via factor analysis of our survey with effective altruist items (Caviola, Althaus, et al., 2022). The six most central items of the effectiveness-focus factor form the effectiveness-focus scale. The participants first read the following text.

> Imagine a situation where you intend to do good (e.g., to improve others' lives or the world) with a certain limited amount of resources available (e.g., your time or money). You can decide how to allocate your resources by choosing from different options that all do good. The stakes are high.

Subsequently, the participants were asked whether they agree or disagree with the following statements. Again, agreement with these items was measured on a scale from 1 (strongly disagree) to 4 (neither agree nor disagree) to 7 (strongly agree).

> In such a situation, when you can choose between different options of doing good,
> - helping one person is less valuable than helping two people to the same extent.
> - the most important consideration is effectiveness—choosing the option that does the most good per resource invested.
> - you should follow evidence and reason to do what is most effective, even if you emotionally prefer another option.
> - it would be the right choice to refrain from helping one person if that makes it possible to help a larger number of people.
> - you should usually help a large group of people over a smaller group, even if it seems unfair.
> - it would be wrong to do something that only does some amount of good if there is an alternative course of action that would do much more good.

We calculated the effectiveness-focus score as the straight average of the responses on the six items. In another of the surveys of the US general population mentioned above (involving 275 participants), we found large individual differences in effectiveness-focus, too. Some people simply disagree, for example, that helping one person is less valuable than helping two; and they are unlikely to find effective altruism appealing. Other participants consistently agreed that the more effective option is better. And many participants were somewhere in-between. Effectiveness-focus scores were normally distributed with a mean of 4.4—that is, the same as the expansive altruism mean score (Caviola, Althaus, et al., 2022).

We also found that effectiveness-focus predicts several effective altruist outcome measures. People who scored higher on the effectiveness-focus scale consistently gave more effectively in charitable giving tasks that involved various obstacles to effective giving. For example, such participants were more likely to help large numbers of statistical victims pitted against a single identifiable victim ($r = .29$). They were also less averse to deprioritizing a less effective option for the sake of a more effective option ($r = .22$) and more likely to choose the option with the higher expected values in a task involving risk ($r = .16$). They didn't have as strong a preference for splitting their donations as other participants, instead often preferring to exclusively prioritize the most effective option when it was clear that splitting would help fewer people ($r = .25$). In short, participants' effectiveness-focus scores robustly predicted effective giving.

Likewise, in the task where participants were asked whether to give money to their favorite charity, to give it to an effective charity helping the world's poorest people, or to keep it for oneself, effectiveness-focus predicted the proportion of participants who prioritized the effective charity over their favorite charity ($r = .26$). On the other hand, it didn't significantly predict how much they were willing to give to either of the charities (as opposed to keeping the money for themselves). This supports the notion that effectiveness-focus specifically measures attitudes to effectiveness (in altruistic contexts) and not level of altruism.

As we saw in the expansive altruism section, participants also read an introductory text about effective altruism and were tested on several additional outcome measures. We found that participants with high effectiveness-focus scores reacted more positively toward the text about effective altruism ($r = .49$), were more interested in learning more about effective altruism ($r = .21$), and were more open to changing their career path to have a higher impact ($r = .19$). By contrast, effectiveness-focus did not predict willingness to sign up for the effective altruism newsletter, willingness to read William MacAskill's (2015) *Doing Good Better* (an introduction to effective altruism), or willingness to donate to effective charities.

We also studied demographic correlations (across all 534 participants) and found that politically liberal ($r = .16$) and younger ($r = .12$) participants scored higher on the effectiveness-focus scale, just like they scored higher on the expansive altruism scale. However, we also found that men tended to score higher on the effectiveness-focus scale ($r = .21$)—in contrast to the expansive altruism scale, where women got higher scores. These demographic correlations were, however, relatively weak—just like those relating to expansive altruism—and need to be researched further.

The effectiveness-focus scale was also included in the survey of New York University students (Caviola, Morrissey, & Lewis, 2022). The mean effectiveness-focus score in this sample was 4.2, slightly lower than the mean score in the sample of the general population (4.4). Moreover, effectiveness-focus scores continued to correlate positively with positive attitudes toward the introductory text about effective altruism ($r = .34$) and interest in learning more about effective altruism ($r = .17$).

We also included the effectiveness-focus scale in the set of items we presented to the previously mentioned sample of 226 effective altruists (Caviola, Althaus, et al., 2022). They had an average score of 6.0, much higher than the scores in the other two samples. Furthermore, we found a correlation ($r = .35$) between how much these participants self-identified with effective altruism and how effectiveness-focused they were. This correlation was about as strong as the correlation between effective altruist self-identification and expansive altruism ($r = .37$), indicating that the two factors are roughly equally strong predictors of real-life engagement with effective altruism. Again, these correlations provide an external form of validation that the two scales measure what they are supposed to measure.

Lastly, and importantly, the survey of New York University students replicated our original survey's finding that expansive altruism and effectiveness-focus are clearly separate psychological constructs. While there was a positive correlation between the two scales both in the sample of the general population ($r = .23$) and in the sample of New York University students ($r = .24$), these correlations weren't particularly strong. Relatedly, only a small fraction of people had a high score on both scales—and to find effective altruism immediately appealing, you may need high scores on both scales. In our sample of the general population, 14.0% of participants had a mean score of 5.0 (equivalent to a slight agreement) or higher on both the expansive altruism and the effectiveness-focus scale, and 3.0% had a mean score of 6.0 (equivalent to agreement) or higher on both scales. In the sample of New York University students, 11.8% of participants had a mean score of 5.0 or higher on both scales, and only 1.7% had a mean score of 6.0 or higher on both scales. By contrast, 81% of participants in our effective altruist sample had a mean score of 5.0 or higher on both scales, and 33% had a mean score of 6.0 or higher on both scales (Caviola, Morrissey, & Lewis, 2022).

Truth-Seeking

Together, expansive altruism and effectiveness-focus predict whether someone is inclined to agree with effective altruism's moral stances. But moral agreement with effective altruism isn't sufficient for acting in line with effective altruism. To apply effective altruism in the real world, additional traits are needed. In particular, effective altruists frequently emphasize the importance of epistemic qualities. Effective altruism is often even defined partially in epistemic terms; for example, part of William MacAskill's definition is "the use of evidence and careful reasoning to work out how to maximize the good with a given unit of resources" (2019, p. 14).

While subscribing to expansive altruism and effectiveness-focus is a good start, it doesn't suffice to actually do good effectively. Finding the most cost-effective charities and the highest-impact careers is very difficult. Many are *cognitive misers* and don't even give it a real try (Stanovich et al., 2016). Others are led astray by motivated reasoning and a host of biases. Even people who believe that one shouldn't prioritize a charity just because it is a personal favorite are often epistemically biased in favor of such charities (Lewis, 2016). They overestimate their effectiveness and thus continue to support them despite evidence that they are not among the most effective charities.

To overcome these biases and find the most effective ways of doing good, we need to cultivate a spirit of honest truth-seeking—what the writer Julia Galef (2021) calls the *scout mindset*. We are naturally inclined toward what Galef calls a *soldier mindset*, meaning that we defend our views whether they're right or wrong (Haidt, 2012; Mercier & Sperber, 2011, 2017). Since the soldier mindset isn't conducive to finding the truth, we should replace it with the scout mindset.

A related psychological construct is *actively open-minded thinking*, which measures people's tendency to want to ground their beliefs in evidence (Baron, 2008; Stanovich & West, 1997). The actively open-minded thinking scale includes the following items (participants are asked to indicate their level of agreement):

- People should take into consideration evidence that goes against conclusions they favor.
- People should revise their conclusions in response to relevant new information.

- Changing your mind is a sign of weakness. (Reversed)
- People should search actively for reasons why they might be wrong.
- It is important to be loyal to your beliefs even when evidence is brought to bear against them. (Reversed)

Actively open-minded thinking is thus a measure of how people think that one ought to think, not a measure of how they actually think. Nevertheless, it has been shown to predict relevant behavior. In a series of studies, Uriel Haran, Ilana Ritov, and Barbara A. Mellers (2013) found that when asked to make estimates and predictions under uncertainty, actively open-minded thinkers collect more information than less actively open-minded people do.

There is also evidence that actively open-minded thinking predicts effective altruist inclinations. Matti Wilks and her colleagues have discovered that members of Giving What We Can (Chapters 3 and 5) are significantly more prone to actively open-minded thinking than the population average. In a study, they found that while the general public's mean score on the actively open-minded thinking scale was 3.65 (on a scale from 1 to 5), Giving What We Can members' mean score was 4.17 (Wilks et al., 2023). That lends some support to the hypothesis that there's a link between actively open-minded thinking and endorsement of effective altruism.

The actively open-minded thinking scale provides a good start for research on epistemic attitudes of importance to effective altruism, but it has its limitations. First, the actively open-minded thinking scale doesn't capture all of the epistemic attitudes and virtues that seem relevant. They may include, for instance, intellectual honesty, intellectual modesty, a willingness to defer to experts, a scientific mindset, an interest in applying economic and statistical reasoning to prosocial contexts, and a desire to figure out uncomfortable truths. Some of these traits may be studied with existing psychological scales—such as the need for cognition construct (Cacioppo & Petty, 1982; Petty et al., 2009), which measures individuals' inclination to engage in effortful cognition—but one may also want to create more tailor-made scales.

Second, it would be useful to have measures of how people actually reason, as opposed to self-reported views on how one should reason. There are, of course, useful tests of raw cognitive ability, but one would also want tests of people's epistemic habits and dispositions—for example, their tendency to change their minds when presented with new evidence. In fact, Keith Stanovich, Richard West, and Maggie Toplak (2016) have developed such a "rationality test"—the Comprehensive Assessment of Rational Thinking

(CART)—which measures a range of epistemic dispositions and abilities. While this research is still in its infancy, and while CART is not specifically geared toward the epistemic virtues of greatest importance to effective altruism, we think it's a good start. It would be useful to pursue more research on these issues and to either refine CART or develop entirely new kinds of measures of sound reasoning. Since truth-seeking and other epistemic virtues are so crucial for the practice of effective altruism, getting a better understanding of them could potentially be very valuable.

Future Research

Besides moral and epistemic features, there are most likely still other features that can predict whether someone will practice effective altruism well. In other research of ours, we have discussed two additional features: collaborativeness and determination (Schubert & Caviola, 2023).

To be *collaborative* means to be willing to coordinate and collaborate with others to maximize our collective impact. It is difficult to have a big impact all alone, even for someone who holds effective altruist moral values and the right epistemic attitudes. We tend to be more effective when working with others. That's why effective altruists have formed a deeply collaborative community. To get the most out of that, it helps to have a collaborative attitude.

By *determination*, we mean, in turn, to apply one's convictions in the real world. Many people have moral values that they don't act upon. They suffer from an intention–behavior gap; that is, they don't translate their intentions into behavior (Sheeran & Webb, 2016). That may prevent them from having much of an impact even if they are expansively altruistic and effectiveness-focused and even if they are diligent truth-seekers. Thus, effective altruism arguably requires a certain level of determination.

However, we have not yet conducted empirical research into the psychological structure of these features, nor have we studied to what extent they predict involvement in effective altruism. It's possible that they are not, in fact, independent psychological factors but that they rather reduce to other factors (cf. our finding that willingness to give away resources to help others and impartiality with regard to close and distant others are to be seen as one and the same factor). We hope that future research could help us to understand these and other features that could be important for the practice of effective altruism.

We also need more in-depth research on how common positive inclinations toward effective altruism are. In the study described above (undertaken in April 2022), we found that only 7.4% of the participants in the sample of New York University students could demonstrate that they clearly understand what effective altruism is, whereas 25% agreed with its key ideas after reading a brief introduction (Caviola, Morrissey, & Lewis, 2022). That gives us some preliminary indication of effective altruism's potential size, but more detailed research is needed. We also want more research on which demographic groups are especially likely to be positively inclined toward effective altruism, for example, where they live and which professions they tend to have. It could be of particular interest to study attitudes toward effective altruism among experts with effective altruism–relevant competence, such as philosophers, economists, public health experts, healthcare practitioners, and policymakers.

Conclusion

Most people find effective altruism unintuitive, due to the many psychological obstacles we covered in Part I. But some take a different view and find effective altruism a promising or even obvious philosophy. We have seen that these people tend to have two sets of moral views in common. First, they are expansive altruists: They are willing to make altruistic sacrifices, including for beneficiaries who are spatially, temporally, and biologically distant from them. Second, they are effectiveness-focused: They are willing to make tough trade-offs to maximize impact, even if that goes against their gut instincts. These factors are not strongly correlated, which means that only a few people have both of them to a high degree. It thus takes an unusual combination of psychological tendencies to be naturally inclined toward effective altruism. (Though this isn't to say that only people with those traits will ever take an interest in effective altruism: As we will see in the next chapter, over time changing norms could attract broader groups.)

In addition to expansive altruism and effectiveness-focus, we also need to have other traits to apply effective altruism well. In particular, we need to have a truth-seeking attitude. Future studies could help us understand what psychological traits make you more effective at helping others. It's an area of research with rich potential.

References

Baron, J. (2008). *Thinking and deciding* (4th ed.). Cambridge University Press.

Cacioppo, J. T., & Petty, R. E. (1982). The need for cognition. *Journal of Personality and Social Psychology, 42*(1), 116–131.

Caviola, L., Althaus, D., Schubert, S., & Lewis, J. (2022, February 25). *What psychological traits predict interest in effective altruism?* Effective Altruism Forum. https://forum.effectivealtruism.org/posts/7f3sq7ZHcRsaBBeMD/what-psychological-traits-predict-interest-in-effective. Additional material can be found at https://osf.io/nh5bc/

Caviola, L., Morrissey, E., & Lewis, J. (2022, May 19). *Most students who would agree with EA ideas haven't heard of EA yet (results of a large-scale survey)*. Effective Altruism Forum. https://forum.effectivealtruism.org/posts/mNRNWkFBZ2K6SHD8a/most-students-who-would-agree-with-ea-ideas-haven-t-heard-of

Crimston, D., Bain, P. G., Hornsey, M. J., & Bastian, B. (2016). Moral expansiveness: Examining variability in the extension of the moral world. *Journal of Personality and Social Psychology, 111*(4), 636–653.

Crimston, C. R., Hornsey, M. J., Bain, P. G., & Bastian, B. (2018). Toward a psychology of moral expansiveness. *Current Directions in Psychological Science, 27*(1), 14–19.

Galef, J. (2021). *The scout mindset: Why some people see things clearly and others don't*. Penguin.

Haidt, J. (2012). *The righteous mind: Why good people are divided by politics and religion*. Pantheon Books.

Haran, U., Ritov, I., & Mellers, B. A. (2013). The role of actively open-minded thinking in information acquisition, accuracy, and calibration. *Judgment and Decision Making, 8*(3), 188–201.

Lewis, G. (2016, January 24). Beware surprising and suspicious convergence. *Gregory Lewis* (blog). https://gregoryjlewis.com/2016/01/24/beware-surprising-and-suspicious-convergence/

MacAskill, W. (2015). *Doing good better: Effective altruism and a radical new way to make a difference*. Guardian Faber Publishing.

MacAskill, W. (2019). The definition of effective altruism. In H. Greaves & T. Pummer (Eds.), *Effective altruism: Philosophical issues* (pp. 10–28). Oxford University Press.

Mercier, H., & Sperber, D. (2011). Why do humans reason? Arguments for an argumentative theory. *The Behavioral and Brain Sciences, 34*(2), 57–74; discussion 74–111.

Mercier, H., & Sperber, D. (2017). *The enigma of reason*. Harvard University Press.

Petty, R. E., Brinol, P., Loersch, C., & McCaslin, M. J. (2009). The need for cognition. In M. R. Leary & R. H. Hoyle (Eds.), *Handbook of individual differences in social behavior* (pp. 318–329). Guilford Press.

Schubert, S., & Caviola, L. (2023). Virtues for real-world utilitarians. In H. Viciana, A. Gaitán, & F. A. González (Eds.), *Experiments in moral and political philosophy* (pp. 163–184). Routledge.

Sheeran, P., & Webb, T. L. (2016). The intention–behavior gap. *Social and Personality Psychology Compass, 10*(9), 503–518.

Singer, P. (1981). *The expanding circle: Ethics and sociobiology*. Clarendon Press.

Stanovich, K. E., & West, R. F. (1997). Reasoning independently of prior belief and individual differences in actively open-minded thinking. *Journal of Educational Psychology, 89*(2), 342–357.

Stanovich, K. E., West, R. F., & Toplak, M. E. (2016). *The rationality quotient: Toward a test of rational thinking*. MIT Press.

Wilks, M., McCurdy, J., & Bloom, P. (2023). Who gives? Characteristics of those who have taken the giving what we can pledge. *Journal of Personality*. Advance online publication. https://doi.org/10.1111/jopy.12842

8
Fundamental Value Change

In the last two chapters, we looked at how we can increase the effectiveness of people's help to others without changing their fundamental values. First, we looked at how we can use nudges, incentives, and the provision of factual information (Chapter 6). Then we looked at how we can identify the effective altruist enthusiasts, who are already positively disposed to effective altruism and therefore may be open to its core message (Chapter 7). An advantage of these strategies is that they are relatively tractable ways of raising the effectiveness of people's help to others.

But at the same time, they have their limits. It's hard to see how these strategies, on their own, could make broader swathes of society adopt more effective approaches in altruistic contexts. Instead, we can only achieve that by changing society's fundamental values: by spreading the message that it's crucial to choose the most effective interventions when helping others. That is a much more challenging project, and it may not succeed fully any time soon. On the other hand, getting only a fraction of society to adopt these values could make a big difference. This chapter will look at strategies aimed at achieving such fundamental value change. We will first look at the efficacy of reason-based moral arguments. Next, we turn to a method that starts out by targeting groups with many effective altruist enthusiasts and uses them as a springboard for spreading effective altruist norms more broadly in society.

Can Moral Arguments Change People's Values?

Effective altruism heavily emphasizes the importance of reason and evidence (Chapter 7; MacAskill, 2017, 2019). Anecdotally, it seems that many early adopters were convinced of effective altruism by reason-based arguments, including philosophical reasoning and empirical evidence of the huge differences in effectiveness between interventions (Chapter 2). Therefore, it's natural to ask whether such arguments could attract broader groups to effective altruism. Could larger parts of society be convinced of the importance of helping others effectively and impartially through reason-based moral arguments?

In the 2022 Effective Altruism Survey, a large fraction of respondents stated that the philosophy of Peter Singer had influenced their decision to embrace effective altruism (Sleegers & Moss, 2023). One of his most famous moral arguments is the drowning child argument that we encountered in Chapter 1 (Singer, 1972). As we saw, Singer argues that if we consider it morally required to save a drowning child out of a pond when we can do so at a small cost to ourselves, then we should also consider it morally required to donate to charity to save the lives of distant people (since that cost is also small). Toby Ord, one of the pioneers of effective altruism, was inspired by this sort of argument when he founded the giving community Giving What We Can (see Chapter 3), whose members pledge to give at least 10% of their income to effective charities (Ord & MacAskill, 2016). As Giving What We Can was one of the first effective altruist organizations, it is particularly noteworthy that moral arguments featured in its genesis.

The drowning child argument is about altruism and helping others in general; the A in EA, as it were (Chapter 7). But the part of effective altruism that we primarily focus on in this book is the effectiveness part: to spend whatever resources one allocates to others effectively. From early on, the effective altruism movement's focus on effectiveness was partially based on the empirical observation that the differences in effectiveness between different ways of helping others are very large (Chapter 2; Jamison et al., 2006). In his paper "The Moral Imperative Toward Cost-Effectiveness in Global Health," Toby Ord (2013) argued that the large differences in cost-effectiveness between different health interventions mean that it is of great moral significance to allocate one's altruistic resources to the most cost-effective interventions.

In addition to this empirical evidence, several philosophers have given sophisticated *a priori* arguments for the importance of effectiveness in altruistic contexts. For instance, in Chapter 1, we saw that Derek Parfit (1982, p. 131) argued that if you could either save both of a man's arms or just one at the same risk for yourself it would be perverse to save just one. In recent years, Theron Pummer and Joe Horton have given structurally similar arguments for the importance of effectiveness in altruistic contexts (Horton, 2017; Pummer, 2016).

How Effective Are Moral Arguments?

Since many of the effective altruism movement's current members were persuaded of effective altruism at least in part by empirical evidence, philosophical reasoning, and other sorts of reason-based arguments, it is only natural to ask how the wider population would react to such arguments. Can they, too, be swayed by reason-based moral arguments?

The last few decades have seen a lot of research on the role of argument and explicit reasoning in human psychology. Notably, much of this research claims that arguments are not particularly reliable and that human cognition relies much more on intuition than people previously thought (Mercier & Sperber, 2011, 2017). According to Jonathan Haidt (2001), it is intuition, rather than reasoned argument, that drives our moral judgments. In his view, reasoning is a feeble "rider" sitting on top of a big "elephant"—our intuitions—that is in charge (Haidt, 2001, 2012; Mercier & Sperber, 2011, 2017). On an extreme version of this view, people only accept arguments that align with their preexisting intuitions, meaning arguments have little independent force. They cannot cause people to alter their fundamental moral worldview, which is rather determined by intuition.

Is this view correct? Or can moral arguments make a difference, as others have argued (Coppock, 2023; Pinillos, 2020)? Let us look at some research on the efficacy of moral arguments that is relevant for effective altruism.

A study by Eric Schwitzgebel and Joshua Rust (2014) showing that moral philosophers don't necessarily behave more ethically than others is sometimes seen as evidence for the inefficacy of moral argument. A possible interpretation of this finding is that it throws doubt on the idea that moral reflection improves behavior (though it should be said that it is complicated to measure the ethical standards of behavior, and more studies on this issue are needed; Hou et al., 2022; Schoenegger & Wagner, 2019). Similarly, Schwitzgebel and Fiery Cushman (2015) found that professional philosophers are just as sensitive to the framing and order of moral dilemmas as laypeople.

But there is also research that has found important effects of moral arguments on behavior. In 2019, Schwitzgebel and Cushman launched a public contest on moral arguments designed to persuade people to donate to charity (Schwitzgebel & Cushman, 2019). Anyone could submit a short argument (no more than 500 words long) appealing to reason (rather than emotion).

Schwitzgebel and Cushman (2020) received around 100 submissions, which they whittled down in successive stages. First, they picked the 20 arguments they found most promising based on their subjective judgment. They then did a light-touch experimental screening of the remaining contenders and let the five best-performing arguments proceed to the final stage, which featured rigorous tests with thousands of participants. The participants were randomly presented with different arguments and subsequently asked whether they wanted to donate up to $10 to charity. They could keep any money they didn't donate for themselves, meaning real personal interests were at stake.

Notably, Schwitzgebel and Cushman found that all five arguments significantly increased the participants' willingness to donate to charity compared with a baseline control condition, where no argument was given. The average donation amounts ranged from $3.32 to $3.98 in the conditions involving the five moral arguments, whereas the average donation amount in the control condition was only $2.58. The largest donations were, on average, given by participants who had read an argument written by the philosophers Peter Singer and Matthew Lindauer (Schwitzgebel & Cushman, 2020):

> Many people in poor countries suffer from a condition called trachoma. Trachoma is the major cause of preventable blindness in the world. Trachoma starts with bacteria that get in the eyes of children, especially children living in hot and dusty conditions where hygiene is poor. If not treated, a child with trachoma bacteria will begin to suffer from blurred vision and will gradually go blind, though this process may take many years. A very cheap treatment is available that cures the condition before blindness develops. As little as $25, donated to an effective agency, can prevent someone going blind later in life.
>
> How much would you pay to prevent your own child becoming blind? Most of us would pay $25,000, $250,000, or even more, if we could afford it. The suffering of children in poor countries must matter more than one-thousandth as much as the suffering of our own child. That's why it is good to support one of the effective agencies that are preventing blindness from trachoma, and need more donations to reach more people.

More recently, Ben Grodeck and Philipp Schoenegger (2023) tested the effect of another moral argument about the importance of charitable giving. The first paragraph described how millions of people live in extreme poverty and explained how much suffering that causes. The second paragraph read as follows:

> People living in Western countries—like you—are, on average, much wealthier than people living in developing countries. Compared to those living in extreme poverty, you have a much greater capacity to help those who are living in extreme poverty.

Grodeck and Schoenegger presented this argument to British participants and found that it had a substantial effect. Participants who were presented with this moral argument were 22-28% more likely to donate money to GiveDirectly than participants in a control condition, who were not presented with any argument. In terms of amounts, participants who had read the argument donated 43-52% more than control condition participants.

Other studies have more explicitly looked at arguments relating to choices between more and less effective helping decisions. One of them is Karen Huang, Joshua Greene, and Max Bazerman's (2019) study of veil of ignorance reasoning, which we encountered in Chapters 3 and 4. They found that if people imagine not knowing their identity, they become more inclined to prioritize effective charities helping distant beneficiaries relative to less effective charities helping American beneficiaries (Harsanyi, 1955; Rawls, 1971). They also found that veil of ignorance reasoning makes people more likely to want to save a greater number of people in a hospital prioritization decision. However, the effect sizes were relatively small, and it is unclear what the long-term effects of these interventions are. That said, this study gives some evidence that reason-based moral arguments can make people more inclined to be more effective in altruistic contexts.

A study of our own gave somewhat more mixed evidence (Caviola & Schubert, 2022). We introduced participants to a principle we called the *save more lives principle*, saying that "one should choose the option that saves more lives" (as opposed to fewer lives) when helping others, and then presented them with examples where one could apply this principle. We found that most participants agreed with the principle in the context of drowning children, where it said that one should prioritize saving 10 children over one child. Most participants also agreed that one should prioritize a more effective malaria charity over a less effective HIV charity, another explicitly stated implication of the principle. However, these findings didn't generalize to other contexts. Participants who had been presented with the save more lives principle were not more inclined than other participants to choose the more effective option in further donation tasks where the save more lives principle wasn't explicitly mentioned. They included a task where an arthritis charity was pitted against a cancer charity (Chapter 1) and a task where a charity supporting an identifiable victim was pitted against a charity supporting a larger number of statistical victims (Chapter 2). In other words, people only applied the save more lives principle when it was explicitly mentioned. They didn't integrate it into their thinking in a deeper way and didn't start to apply it more generally.

How do arguments that appeal to reason compare with arguments that appeal to emotion? As we've seen, psychologists like Jonathan Haidt (2001, 2012) have argued that moral judgment is primarily driven by intuition and emotion. That might suggest that emotion-based arguments should work better than reason-based arguments. Is that the case? To study that issue, a team of philosophers and psychologists—Matthew Lindauer, Marcus Mayorga, Joshua Greene, Paul Slovic, Daniel Västfjäll, and Peter Singer (2020)—conducted an experiment that pitted a reason-based and an emotional argument for charitable donations against each other. The reason-based argument was based on the drowning child argument but also featured a so-called evolutionary debunking argument, saying that we feel more for nearby victims than for distant victims for evolutionary reasons that lack moral significance (Chapter 3). The emotional argument, in turn, featured a photo and a short description of a single identifiable victim (see Chapter 2).

The study didn't yield any conclusive results either way. The researchers found that both arguments significantly increased donations, but there wasn't a significant difference in donation amounts between the group that read the reason-based argument and the group that read the emotion-based argument. Similarly, giving both arguments didn't increase donations significantly compared to giving one of them.

One general issue with the studies of moral arguments we have discussed so far is that they are quite artificial. Participants are recruited online, presented with a short moral argument, and subsequently asked whether or where they would like to donate. This is quite unlike how people normally interact with moral arguments in their daily life. Thus, it is unclear how these findings transfer to the real world. Ideally, we want more ecologically valid studies that test the effects of moral argument in real-world settings.

So far, there aren't too many such studies, but there are some examples, such as Eric Schwitzgebel, Bradford Cokelet, and Peter Singer's (2020) recent paper on the effectiveness of ethics classes "in the wild." They divided over 1000 University of California philosophy students into two groups: one which was taught the ethics of charitable giving and one which was taught the ethics of meat-eating. For one week, the two groups were presented with different reading materials and content (they had the same content the rest of the semester). The charitable giving group read an article by Peter Singer (1999) arguing that luxurious spending is immoral and that we are morally required to donate to help people in poverty. They were also encouraged to watch a video advocating for charitable giving to relieve hunger. The ethics of meat-eating group rather read an article by James Rachels (2004) arguing that it's unethical to eat meat. They were also encouraged to watch a video that contained footage of factory farms as part of an argument for vegetarianism. In addition, students discussed their assigned topics with each other and teaching assistants during a 50-minute discussion session. Thus, the study was similar to how university ethics courses are usually taught.

After the students had taken the course, they were surveyed on their attitudes to charitable giving and meat-eating. The results were notably mixed. Students who had been taught the ethics of charitable giving were not more likely to want to avoid luxurious spending than students in the other group. In fact, they were less likely to do so, meaning that it is possible that the teaching on the ethics of charitable giving had a "backfire effect."

On the other hand, teaching the ethics of meat-eating did have an effect. Whereas 29% of the students who had been taught the ethics of charitable giving agreed that eating the meat of factory-farmed animals is unethical, 43% of the students who had been taught the ethics of meat-eating had that view by the end of the semester. Moreover, these differences in attitudes were mirrored by differences in behavior. Before the intervention, the two groups bought meat in the student cafeteria with the same frequency: 52% (of purchases worth at least $4.99). Among students who had been taught the ethics of charitable giving, that number remained the same after the intervention; but among students who had been taught the ethics of meat-eating, the rate had fallen to 45%. These findings were replicated in a later study, suggesting that the effects are relatively robust (Schwitzgebel et al., 2021). They are striking because they suggest that a fairly basic intervention involving ethics teaching can change people's moral behavior. However, as always, it's not obvious how well the findings generalize. More studies on a wider range of scenarios could be very valuable.

Are Moral Arguments Enough?

The contemporary literature on the effects of moral arguments on charitable giving and related forms of behavior is relatively small. The evidence from the studies we have covered is mixed. On the one hand, some studies have found that reason-based moral arguments can make a difference. On the other hand, the effects don't tend to be very large. There are also questions regarding how well these studies transfer to the real world and whether behavioral changes last over the longer term. Lastly, with only a few exceptions such as the paper by Huang, Greene, and Bazerman (2019), studies of moral arguments have not focused on whether one should be effective when helping others. Instead, they have focused on other issues, such as whether and how much to help others. We need more studies that focus specifically on arguments relating to effectiveness. In particular, studies on attitudes to effectiveness that employ more comprehensive interventions than brief online arguments could be useful. For instance, it could be useful to study the effects of teaching semester-long courses with a variety of didactic tools. Though such more ambitious interventions would be more costly—both at the research stage and when the interventions are finally rolled out—they could be especially effective.

In any event, so far we've not found evidence to suggest that giving reason-based arguments would by itself sway people to help effectively on a large scale. Another reason to be skeptical of that is that if such arguments made a huge difference, one would have expected more people to have become effective altruists by now. After all, effective altruists have given plenty of reason-based arguments for more than a decade, and the effective altruism movement is still relatively small.

Arguments and Norms Interact

In light of these findings, one might think that effective altruism is unlikely to become very popular. It is probably true that most people won't accept the key ideas of effective altruism in the short run. They just won't be swayed by its arguments. However, in the longer run, it's at least possible that effective altruism could grow more substantially, thanks to two facts: the individual differences in inclination toward effective altruism and the power of norms. Let's look at these two factors in turn.

Even though most people find the core claims of effective altruism unintuitive, some are more positively disposed to them. These are the effective altruism enthusiasts we discussed in Chapter 7: people who are inclined to help others, including distant others, at a personal cost, and who are willing to accept tough trade-offs for greater effectiveness. Many of them likely accept effective altruism when they are exposed to its arguments.

So far, effective altruism has likely been especially successful among these people, who are naturally inclined to accept its ideas. It may be harder to grow among groups who are intuitively more skeptical of effective altruism. However, some features of human psychology may make it more likely: in particular, the way we're influenced by norms and what our peers think. Humans are norm-following: We have expectations of how people will and should behave, which greatly influence our own behavior (Bicchieri, 2005; Gross & Vostroknutov, 2022).

As we saw in Chapter 1, social norms are part of the reason that most altruistic efforts currently aren't very effective. Most people think that if they feel strongly about a particular charity, it's right and appropriate for them to prioritize that charity, even if it turns out to be less effective than the alternatives. Moreover, they think that others should do so as well. In this sense, there is a norm against effective altruism.

That norm is part of the reason that effective altruism is so uncommon. However, it would likely weaken if more people were to adopt effective altruism. Today, most people exclusively have peers who support the norm that runs counter to effective altruism. They don't have any family members, friends, or colleagues who believe in alternative norms that are more aligned with effective altruism. But the growing number of effective altruists could lead to more people having at least some peers who believe in effective altruist ideas. For those people, the norms would be more ambiguous. The barrier to adoption of effective altruism would be lowered. They would get conflicting messages from different parts of their peer group. There could even be some people who mostly have peers who follow and support effective altruist norms. They would naturally be much more inclined to adopt such norms themselves. The tables could thus be turned: For some people, peer effects could make people more, rather than less, likely to endorse effective altruism. Consequently, people subject to those reversed peer effects could come to endorse effective altruism as well, further increasing the chance that still other people do so. These kinds of self-reinforcing processes ("norm cascades") can be very powerful (Cialdini, 1985; Sunstein, 2019).

The economist Robert H. Frank (2021) cites several cases of such "behavioral contagion," as he calls it, in his book *Under the Influence: Putting Peer Pressure to Work*. A prominent example is attitudes toward same-sex marriage. In 2009, only 40% of Americans supported same-sex marriage; but by 2018, that number had increased to two-thirds (McCarthy, 2018). Attitudes shifted quickly, in part because it became seen as more acceptable to support same-sex marriage and less acceptable not to. As recently as 2008, Barack Obama and Hillary Clinton were against it, whereas today it would be seen as highly problematic not to support it in many circles (Frank, 2021).

Historically, behavioral contagion has contributed to social sea changes. Many ideas we now take for granted were once weak and impeded by powerful norms. Before the Scientific Revolution, the idea that we ought to understand the world through impartial empirical research was not nearly as popular as it is today. It only gained ground slowly and gradually—but eventually, it conquered (Mokyr, 2016). The same was true of the moral and political ideals of the Enlightenment, such as religious tolerance and political liberty. Yet another example is racial equality, which was long opposed in much of society. In 1958, only 4% of Americans approved of interracial marriage. Since then, change has been fast, however: In 2021, 94% approved of it (McCarthy, 2021).

Could something similar happen to effective altruism? Could our current norms—that we should support whatever charity or cause we prefer, even if that reduces effectiveness—be replaced by norms that celebrate effectiveness?

It is hard to say. One reason to think that effective altruism could spread is that it's built on ideas like the scientific mindset and moral impartiality, which have become progressively more popular over the course of history. We may have inductive reasons to think that those ideas will continue to become more popular—and, with them, effective altruism.

Another reason to think that effective altruism may spread relates to cultural evolution (Henrich, 2015). The most straightforward way of applying effective altruism is through doing good ourselves, for example, by donating to an effective charity. But, as we will see in Chapter 9, people can also have a high impact through sharing knowledge about the principles of effective altruism with others—if they, in turn, become more effective in altruistic contexts. That way, they can, in effect, multiply their impact. Indeed, effective altruists may be unusually inclined to use this strategy since other groups may be averse to such more indirect way of having an impact (Chapter 5). Through this logic, one might expect effective altruism to spread exactly because spreading effective altruism can be an effective way of doing good (Duda, 2020).

On the other hand, there are also some reasons against believing that effective altruism will become a society-wide norm any time soon. Several of the successful movements we've discussed—such as those fighting for same-sex marriage and racial equality—have very salient injustices to point to. We can observe discrimination occurring here and now, in our own society. By contrast, many of the groups that effective altruists support—like the global poor, animals, and future generations—are distant and less salient. That probably makes a powerful norm cascade in support of them less likely. Likewise, the abstract idea of effectiveness is probably not the most emotionally engaging message. That may reduce the chance of a powerful norm cascade further. Exactly how we should weigh these considerations against each other is not easy to say.

Conclusion

Since effective altruism is based on reason and evidence, it is only natural to look at reason-based moral arguments when considering how effective altruism might spread. However, it is unclear how effective moral arguments are. More research is needed, but in general, it seems safe to say that people are not always open to new and original moral ideas, even if they have seemingly compelling arguments. This means that people trying to spread effective altruism may be well advised to start by trying to reach the subset of the population that finds its core claims intuitive. They include intellectually open people who want to help others, including distant others, at a personal cost, and who realize the importance of effectiveness. Once those people are onboard, peer effects working against effective altruism could be reduced or even reversed. That could replicate a process we have seen regarding many other ideas that once were unpopular but eventually won widespread endorsement, such as same-sex marriage and racial equality. However, it remains to be seen whether effective altruism could be as successful as they've been.

References

Bicchieri, C. (2005). *The grammar of society: The nature and dynamics of social norms.* Cambridge University Press.

Caviola, L., & Schubert, S. (2022). *Moral arguments for effective giving fail to change donation behavior* [Unpublished manuscript]. Department of Psychology, Harvard University.

Cialdini, R. B. (1985). *Influence: Science and practice.* Pearson Scott Foresman.

Coppock, A. (2023). *Persuasion in parallel: How information changes minds about politics.* University of Chicago Press.

Duda, R. (2020, July). *Building effective altruism.* 80,000 Hours. Retrieved January 28, 2024 from https://80000hours.org/problem-profiles/promoting-effective-altruism/

Frank, R. H. (2021). *Under the influence: Putting peer pressure to work.* Princeton University Press.

Grodeck, B., & Schoenegger, P. (2023). Demanding the morally demanding: Experimental evidence on the effects of moral arguments and moral demandingness on charitable giving. *Journal of Behavioral and Experimental Economics, 103,* Article 101988.

Gross, J., & Vostroknutov, A. (2022). Why do people follow social norms? *Current Opinion in Psychology, 44,* 1–6.

Haidt, J. (2001). The emotional dog and its rational tail: A social intuitionist approach to moral judgment. *Psychological Review, 108*(4), 814–834.

Haidt, J. (2012). *The righteous mind: Why good people are divided by politics and religion.* Knopf Doubleday Publishing Group.

Harsanyi, J. C. (1955). Cardinal welfare, individualistic ethics, and interpersonal comparisons of utility. *The Journal of Political Economy, 63*(4), 309–321.

Henrich, J. (2015). *The secret of our success.* Princeton University Press.

Horton, J. (2017). The all or nothing problem. *The Journal of Philosophy, 114*(2), 94–104.

Hou, T., Ding, X., & Yu, F. (2022). The moral behavior of ethics professors: A replication-extension in Chinese mainland. *Philosophical Psychology.* Advance online publication. https://doi.org/10.1080/09515089.2022.2084057

Huang, K., Greene, J. D., & Bazerman, M. (2019). Veil-of-ignorance reasoning favors the greater good. *Proceedings of the National Academy of Sciences of the United States of America, 116*(48), 23989–23995.

Jamison, D. T., Breman, J. G., Measham, A. R., Alleyne, G., Claeson, M., Evans, D. B., Jha, P., Mills, A., & Musgrove, P. (2006). *Disease control priorities in developing countries.* World Bank Publications.

Lindauer, M., Mayorga, M., Greene, J. D., Slovic, P., Västfjäll, D., & Singer, P. (2020). Comparing the effect of rational and emotional appeals on donation behavior. *Judgment and Decision Making, 15*(3), 413–420.

MacAskill, W. (2017). Effective altruism: Introduction. *Essays in Philosophy, 18*(1), 1–5.

MacAskill, W. (2019). The definition of effective altruism. In H. Greaves & T. Pummer (Eds.), *Effective altruism: Philosophical issues* (pp. 10–28). Oxford University Press.

McCarthy, J. (2018, May 23). *Two in three Americans support same-sex marriage.* Gallup. https://news.gallup.com/poll/234866/two-three-americans-support-sex-marriage.aspx

McCarthy, J. (2021, September 10). *U.S. approval of interracial marriage at new high of 94%*. Gallup. https://news.gallup.com/poll/354638/approval-interracial-marriage-new-high.aspx

Mercier, H., & Sperber, D. (2011). Why do humans reason? Arguments for an argumentative theory. *The Behavioral and Brain Sciences, 34*(2), 57–74; discussion 74–111.

Mercier, H., & Sperber, D. (2017). *The enigma of reason*. Harvard University Press.

Mokyr, J. (2016). *A culture of growth: The origins of the modern economy*. Princeton University Press.

Ord, T. (2013, March 8). *The moral imperative toward cost-effectiveness in global health*. Center for Global Development. https://cgdev.org/publication/moral-imperative-toward-cost-effectiveness-global-health

Ord, T., & MacAskill, W. (2016, August 31). *Opening keynote* [Conference presentation]. EA Global, San Francisco, CA, United States. Available at https://forum.effectivealtruism.org/posts/9K8Yiv9Fdm7XNsmCm/toby-ord-and-will-macaskill-opening-keynote-2016

Parfit, D. (1982). Future generations: Further problems. *Philosophy & Public Affairs, 11*(2), 113–172.

Pinillos, N. Á. (2020, November 11). *Why arguments still work*. Medium. https://medium.com/curious/why-arguments-still-work-8a387c514ff7

Pummer, T. (2016). Whether and where to give. *Philosophy & Public Affairs, 44*(1), 77–95.

Rachels, J. (2004). The basic argument for vegetarianism. In S. Sapontzis (Ed.), *Food for thought: The debate over eating meat* (pp. 70–80). Prometheus Books.

Rawls, J. (1971). *A theory of justice*. Belknap Press.

Schoenegger, P., & Wagner, J. (2019). The moral behavior of ethics professors: A replication-extension in German-speaking countries. *Philosophical Psychology, 32*(4), 532–559.

Schwitzgebel, E., Cokelet, B., & Singer, P. (2020). Do ethics classes influence student behavior? Case study: Teaching the ethics of eating meat. *Cognition, 203*, Article 104397.

Schwitzgebel, E., Cokelet, B., & Singer, P. (2021). Students eat less meat after studying meat ethics. *Review of Philosophy and Psychology, 14*, 113–138.

Schwitzgebel, E., & Cushman, F. (2015). Philosophers' biased judgments persist despite training, expertise and reflection. *Cognition, 141*, 127–137.

Schwitzgebel, E., & Cushman, F. (2019, October 24). Philosophy contest: Write a philosophical argument that convinces research participants to donate to charity. *The Splintered Mind: Reflections in Philosophy of Psychology, Broadly Construed* (blog). http://schwitzsplinters.blogspot.com/2019/10/philosophy-contest-write-philosophical.html

Schwitzgebel, E., & Cushman, F. (2020, June 23). Contest winner! A philosophical argument that effectively convinces research participants to donate to charity. *The Splintered Mind: Reflections in Philosophy of Psychology, Broadly Construed* (blog). http://schwitzsplinters.blogspot.com/2020/06/contest-winner-philosophical-argument.html

Schwitzgebel, E., & Rust, J. (2014). The moral behavior of ethics professors: Relationships among self-reported behavior, expressed normative attitude, and directly observed behavior. *Philosophical Psychology, 27*(3), 293–327.

Singer, P. (1972). Famine, affluence, and morality. *Philosophy & Public Affairs, 1*(3), 229–243.

Singer, P. (1999, September 5). The Singer solution to world poverty. *The New York Times Magazine*, 60–63. https://www.nytimes.com/1999/09/05/magazine/the-singer-solution-to-world-poverty.html

Sleegers, W., & Moss, D. (2023, July 21). *EA survey 2022: How people get involved in EA*. Effective Altruism Forum. https://forum.effectivealtruism.org/posts/aTSoxTcSjyBWem3Xz/ea-survey-2022-how-people-get-involved-in-ea

Sunstein, C. R. (2019). *How change happens*. MIT Press.

9
Effective Altruism for Mortals

In the last few chapters, we have discussed what one can do to increase the level of effectiveness in altruistic contexts on a societal level. In other words, we've looked at how we can help other people to increase the effectiveness of their altruistic efforts. In this final chapter, we rather ask how individuals who have become convinced of the effective altruist message can apply it in their own lives. What concrete actions should they take? What causes and strategies should they prioritize? And what virtues should they cultivate? Let us now look at these questions.

The Two-Budget Strategy

Some argue that effective altruism entails working constantly, sacrificing friendships and things we do for our personal pleasure, and giving away almost all of our resources to people who have greater needs than ourselves (Nielsen, 2022). But we disagree with that view.

One argument that some defend is that ethics simply isn't that demanding: that people under normal circumstances have a right to spend their money and time as they see fit (Williams, 1985; Wolf, 1982). But regardless of whether one accepts that, working all the time and giving away almost all resources can be psychologically unsustainable and increase the risk of burnout. Relatedly, few people would be interested in joining such a demanding project. Ultimately, that would make effective altruism less effective. Thus, such levels of sacrifice are likely self-defeating. While philosophers debate whether we are still in some sense obligated to live up to such exacting standards, from a practical point of view, it seems wiser to set standards that we're actually able to live up to (Timmerman & Cohen, 2019). As Max Bazerman argues in his book *Better, Not Perfect* (2020), that will, in the end, make us more effective—even though it may not seem so at first glance. With Bazerman's words, we should aim for "maximum sustainable goodness" rather than perfection.

Effective Altruism and the Human Mind. Stefan Schubert and Lucius Caviola, Oxford University Press.
© Oxford University Press 2024. DOI: 10.1093/oso/9780197757376.003.0010

But how should we go about achieving maximum sustainable goodness in practice? How can we find a good balance between the effective altruist goal of maximizing positive impact and our psychological limitations? We have many preferences and desires that don't involve altruistic impact, and we neither can nor should steamroll over them.

One appealing approach is what we call the *two-budget strategy* (Effective Altruism Forum, n.d.a; Wise, 2015). The strategy is to divide our resources—in particular our money—into two budgets: one dedicated to effective altruist purposes and one that we use for everything else.

The resources in the first budget are earmarked for whatever strategies that do the most good in the world. That is, when we're using this budget, we try our best to prioritize the most effective options from a global, impartial, and cause-neutral perspective. Thus, this budget isn't compromising on effective altruism. We won't let our decisions about how to allocate these resources be affected by our personal preferences and desires.

On the other hand, we can use the resources in the second budget however we wish: on ourselves and our hobbies and interests, our loved ones, or whatever else we want to spend them on. This way, we make an explicit decision about how much to spend on effective altruism and how much to spend to satisfy all our other needs and desires.

But what fraction of our resources should we allocate to the effective altruism budget? That is a very difficult question. There's no consensus among philosophers on the difficult question of how demanding morality is—how much we owe to others (Railton, 1984; Singer, 1972; Sobel, 2020; Tanyi & Bruder, 2014; Williams, 1985; Wolf, 1982). And, as we've seen, there's also the complex psychological question of what standards we'd be able to live up to. While we don't have a general answer to how much to allocate to the effective altruism budget, everyone should consider this question carefully. Many effective altruists take the Giving What We Can Pledge and donate 10% of their income to effective causes, but others choose a different number. Everyone has to figure out for themselves what they are comfortable with. It depends on a host of factors, including how old you are, your income, whether you have any dependents, and much else. What's important is that you don't just drift into a level of helping but that you make an explicit decision about it. Some people are constantly thinking that they should do more to help others, making every little decision a negotiation between different parts of themselves, as it were (Singer, 2015; Wise, 2015). That may not be sustainable in the long run. Instead, it seems better to explicitly decide how much to put in the effective altruism budget, say once a year. You do your part to make the world better through the effective altruism budget, meaning that whenever you use your second budget, you don't have to think about effective altruist considerations. Instead, you can spend your resources however you like. The two-budget strategy is thus a compromise between your competing preferences that allows you to have an impact in a psychologically sustainable way.

But psychological sustainability is an important consideration for all our altruistic decisions, not just our donation decisions. In particular, it's an important consideration when we use our time to do good. However, it can be more complex to partition our time than it is to partition our money. In particular, spending a fraction of your time volunteering to help others (analogously to spending a fraction of your money on effective donations) is often not very effective, as we saw in Chapter 5.

But even though we need to think a bit differently when we spend our time compared to when we spend our money, we can still apply a broadly similar mindset. Just as some people feel that they have to donate almost all of their money, some people may feel that they have to work almost all the time to maximize their impact. Others might feel that they have to choose a job they actively dislike to become more effective. In effect, there is a risk that they neglect their own well-being in a naive quest for impact, something that can lead to burnout or depression. Instead, it seems better not to work more than is sustainable and to choose a satisfying job. If we don't do that, our attempts to maximize impact may backfire.

Avoiding the Half-Measure Fallacy

Some people may find that they don't want to stop supporting some less effective cause entirely—for example, because it carries a personal significance for them—even though they are convinced by effective altruism. The two-budget strategy suggests that resources allocated in this way should be taken from the second budget (Yudkowsky, 2009).

This is a useful strategy because it lets us avoid a frequent fallacy, which we call the *half-measure fallacy*: an intuitive but suboptimal compromise between preferences for effectiveness and preferences for personally appealing causes or charities. Suppose that a donor cares about effectiveness but also wants to support a cause that is dear to their heart. Furthermore, suppose that this cause isn't among the most effective causes. How can they strike a compromise between these two preferences?

A potential solution that may come to mind is to stick to the less effective cause but find the most effective charity specializing in that cause. At first glance, that might sound like a good idea. However, as we shall see, it is often rather a suboptimal half-measure.

The reason this is a suboptimal strategy stems from the big differences in effectiveness between different causes and charities. Some causes are much more effective than others (Duda, 2023; Todd, 2021a). Only a small number of charities working on high-impact causes are highly effective, whereas the others are much less effective (Chapter 2). This has important implications for what compromise solutions to select.

To continue our example, suppose that the most effective charity addressing the donor's favorite cause is 10 times more effective than the charity they originally supported but that the most effective charity in the world is 10 times more effective still (Figure 9.1). Under those circumstances, our donor would increase their impact 10 times by switching to the most effective charity addressing their favorite cause, but they could have increased their impact 10 times more if they had switched to the most effective charity in the world. In other words, by choosing the most effective charity addressing their favorite cause they only realize 10% of their potential impact. Thus, this approach only takes them a small fraction of the distance from the effectiveness of their original choice to the effectiveness of the highest-impact charity they could support. That means that it is a suboptimal half-measure. It is much less effective than one might naively think. This is an important point that is not always appreciated even among those who otherwise see the importance of effectiveness.

The two-budget strategy is a much better compromise. Suppose our donor puts half of their donations in their effective altruist budget and the other half in the budget they spend as they feel like. They then allocate the money in the first budget to the most effective charity in the world and the money in the second budget to the charity they originally supported. Since the most effective charity in the world is 100 times more effective than the charity they originally donated to, this strategy will increase their impact approximately 50 times. This means that they will go approximately halfway to their maximum potential impact. In this example, this is roughly five times greater an impact than the half-measure strategy achieves. While that number will vary, the two-budget strategy generally does much better than the half-measure

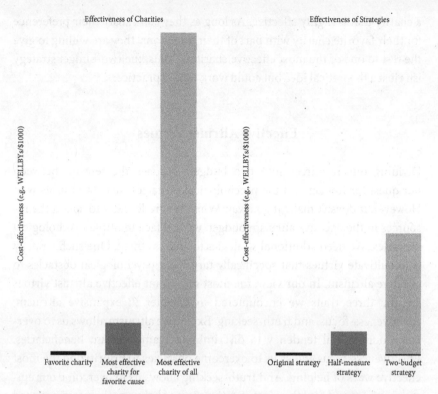

Figure 9.1 The Half-Measure Strategy Versus the Two-Budget Strategy
Note: The left graph shows the effectiveness of the charity the donor originally preferred, the most effective charity working on that cause, and the most effective charity of all. The right graph shows the effectiveness of three strategies for giving: the original strategy (giving to the first charity), the half-measure strategy (giving to the second charity), and the two-budget strategy (giving one-half to the first charity and one-half to the third). WELLBYs = well-being-adjusted life years.

strategy, thanks to the fact that it allocates at least some funds to charities that are dramatically much more effective than the alternatives. It's because the differences in charity effectiveness are so large that it's better to give at least some funds to the very best charities than to give your whole donation to a somewhat effective charity.

As some readers may have noticed, we have already in effect encountered the two-budget strategy in the form of the donation bundling approach that the Giving Multiplier donation platform uses (Chapter 6). In the donation bundling studies discussed in Chapter 6, we found empirical support for the practical feasibility of the two-budget strategy. Many people like to split their donations between a charity that fully satisfies their personal preferences and a charity that is highly effective. As long as they can satisfy their preference for their favorite charity with part of their donations, they are willing to give the rest to one of the most effective charities. Thus, the two-budget strategy isn't just a theoretical idea but could work well in practice.

Effective Altruist Virtues

Dividing our resources into two budgets reduces the tension between our quest for impact and the psychological obstacles that stand in its way. However, it doesn't make it go away. When we are looking to spend the resources in the effective altruism budget, we still face multiple psychological obstacles. We need additional strategies to address them. One such strategy is to cultivate virtues that specifically target key psychological obstacles to effective altruism. In our view, the most important effective altruist virtues are the three traits we encountered in Chapter 7: expansive altruism, effectiveness-focus, and truth-seeking. Expansive altruism allows us to overcome our natural tendency to discriminate against distant beneficiaries. Effectiveness-focus allows us to overcome obstacles to prioritizing the most effective ways of helping. And truth-seeking allows us to overcome our epistemic biases and find the most effective ways of helping. Therefore, we need to cultivate these traits as virtues.

In addition to these core virtues, effective altruists often emphasize additional virtues (Chapter 7). For instance, since it is important to actually follow through with our plans to maximize impact, effective altruists tend to celebrate the virtue of determination, expressed by the slogan "figure out how to do the most good, and *then do it*" (Galef, 2020; our emphasis). Likewise, since it is important to collaborate with other effective altruists to maximize impact, we need the virtue of collaborativeness. Thus, there is a whole package of virtues that effective altruists need to maximize their impact in light of all the psychological obstacles we've identified.

Importantly, effective altruists also need virtues emphasized by common-sense ethics, such as honesty, trustworthiness, and kindness. A naive interpretation of effective altruism might lead someone to believe that it is justified to lie or steal for the greater good. However, this interpretation is wrong. Of course, most people reject such behavior intuitively or as a matter of principle. But even from a strict impact point of view, common-sense virtues like honesty, trustworthiness, and kindness are critical (Schubert & Caviola, 2023). People count on others to follow laws and norms. Lying and stealing for the supposed greater good would cause social trust—a vital component of a good society—to decrease (MacAskill et al., 2023). Moreover, it could have huge reputational costs for effective altruism, which in turn could lead to fewer effective altruists and lower overall impact.

Therefore, it's not true that effective altruists should abandon these common-sense virtues. That would be tantamount to naive effective altruism. The effective altruist virtues of expansive altruism, effectiveness-focus, and truth-seeking do not replace the common-sense virtues but are additions to them. The failure to see this is a dangerous misconception that is important to avoid since it can cause substantial harm.

Finding the Highest-Impact Causes

Having thus looked at what mindset and virtues effective altruists should have, let us now turn to what causes or global problems to prioritize. Since these issues fall outside the book's core focus—the psychology of effective altruism—our summary of them will be brief. Readers who want to learn more are referred to William MacAskill's *Doing Good Better* (2015), The Centre for Effective Altruism's (2023) *Introduction to effective altruism program syllabus*, or one of the books on specific causes that we cover below.

As we saw in Chapter 1, effective altruists argue that we shouldn't prejudge what cause to prioritize but should instead be cause-neutral. In other words, we should choose causes based on impartial assessments of impact rather than on, for example, personal connections. But finding the highest-impact causes is an enormously complicated research problem. The available causes span from local homelessness to improving political institutions to mitigating risks from future technologies. While it's true that metrics such as well-being-adjusted life years (WELLBYs) per $1000 provide us with the theoretical tools we need to compare all kinds of causes (Chapter 5), it's not easy to do so in practice (Layard & Oparina, 2021). Therefore, effective altruists have developed intuitive heuristics such as the scale–tractability–neglectedness framework, according to which a cause's or problem's impact is a function of the following (Wiblin, 2019):

- How much better the world would be if the problem were solved, wholly or in part (Scale)
- How easy it is to make progress on the problem (Tractability)

- How large resources are already being invested in the problem—since our impact will typically be greater if only small amounts of resources are currently invested in it (Neglectedness)

It can be easier to assess causes using this framework than by directly estimating the impact in WELLBYs/$1000. For instance, if a cause does well on all three criteria, we can infer that it has a high impact, even if we don't know the number of WELLBYs it creates per $1000 with any precision. Moreover, this framework can be very helpful when we are looking to judge the relative impact of different causes. For instance, if Cause A is better than Cause B on at least one criterion, and no worse on the others, then Cause A is likely to have a higher impact than Cause B. And usually, such relative judgments are all we need. We don't need to know a cause's absolute impact to prioritize it over another cause. We just need to know that it has a higher impact.

In recent years, cause prioritization, or *global priorities research* as it is often called, has grown as an area of research. One of the largest effective altruist organizations is Open Philanthropy, which recommends grants worth hundreds of millions of dollars per year to high-impact causes (Berger, 2022). Open Philanthropy carefully researches the relative effectiveness of different causes to inform these grant recommendations.

Global priorities research is also undertaken at academic institutes, such as the Global Priorities Institute at the University of Oxford. They conduct foundational research to inform the decision-making of individuals and institutions seeking to increase their positive impact. Their research agenda includes ethical questions about the value of potential future individuals, decision-theoretic questions about how to act under deep uncertainty, and a host of related questions (Greaves et al., 2020).

Much of the effective altruist research consists of detailed empirical studies of individual causes. Let's now turn to the most popular causes in effective altruism: global poverty and health, animal welfare, and the long-term future.

Global Poverty and Health

As we saw in Chapter 3, from early on many effective altruists have focused on global poverty and health. Though the world has seen a lot of progress and poverty has been reduced, there are still almost 700 million people in the world living in extreme poverty (i.e., on less than $2.15 a day) (World Bank, 2023). And yet, relatively small donations are directed toward international causes (Chapter 3; Global Philanthropy Tracker, 2023). That means that global poverty is both large in scale and highly neglected. Moreover, it is also tractable: As we saw in Chapter 2, there are multiple effective and evidence-based interventions that we can use to help the global poor. More funding will save more lives with an unusually high degree of certainty. According to GiveWell's 2021 estimate, the most effective charities they have investigated can save a life for $3500-$5500 (GiveWell, 2023a).

But not everyone agrees that the evidence-based interventions used by GiveWell-recommended charities—for example, distribution of bed nets (Against Malaria Foundation) or supplements to prevent vitamin A deficiency (Helen Keller International)—are the best ways to help the global poor (GiveWell, 2023b). While it is relatively straightforward to gather data on the effectiveness of such interventions, some argue that other approaches, whose effectiveness is harder to measure, are more effective. In particular, they argue that it could be more promising to try to shape government policy. There is a lively debate on these issues in effective altruism (Hillebrandt & Halstead, 2020; Pritchett, 2020).

Readers who want to learn more about effective altruist approaches to global poverty and health are referred to William MacAskill's *Doing Good Better* (2015), which discusses these approaches at length.

Animal Welfare

Animal welfare is another of the core long-standing effective altruist causes (Thomas, 2023). In particular, many effective altruists focus on improving conditions at factory farms, where billions of animals live under appalling conditions. This cause is thus large in scale, and yet it is also relatively neglected as only a fraction of a percent of total US donations go toward farm animals (Chapter 3; Anderson, 2018; Animal Charity Evaluators, 2024).

Moreover, it is also tractable since there are several promising strategies that address harms to farm animals. One common strategy is to try to influence companies that make use of animal products. Animal activists have persuaded companies such as Burger King and McDonald's to commit to using cage-free chicken and eggs (Albert Schweitzer Foundation,

2020; Banker, 2016; Wiblin & Harris, 2021). A related strategy is to target politicians and policymakers and lobby for stricter animal welfare legislation. The effective altruist charity evaluator Animal Charity Evaluators (n.d.) ranks The Humane League, which uses such strategies, as among the most effective charities helping animals.

An entirely different approach—pursued, for example, by the large global charity the Good Food Institute—is to encourage individuals to consume fewer animal products by creating appealing alternatives. These alternative products fall into two categories. The first is plant-based products, for example, almond milk, soy milk, and oat milk; vegan cheese from cashews or soybeans; and tofu as a meat replacement. These products are fairly straightforward to produce and thus relatively cheap. While they don't always taste exactly like the animal products they replace, they have improved over the years; and more funding for product development could lead to further improvements (Good Food Institute, n.d.).

A second approach is to try to produce real meat, milk, cheese, egg white, yolk, and so on, but to do so in a lab, using cell cultures. Scientists have already been able to produce such products, but at first, they were expensive and didn't taste particularly good. When the world's first cultivated meat burger was made in 2013, it cost no less than $325,000 (Fountain, 2013). However, prices are falling, and taste is improving. The Good Food Institute (n.d.) hopes that these products will eventually improve to a point where they become competitive with regular animal products. It should be emphasized, however, that it will likely take time before we see cultivated meat in our convenience stores.

The Long-Term Future

As we saw in Chapter 3, a growing number of effective altruists have come to endorse longtermism (Greaves & MacAskill, 2021; MacAskill, 2022). They think the future could become very long and that it would be enormously valuable to ensure that it becomes as good as it could potentially be. Based on such reasoning, they believe that the long-term future cause is huge in scale.

It is also clearly very neglected since only small numbers of people focus on affecting the future beyond the next few decades or centuries. But a common objection to trying to influence the long-term future is that it isn't tractable: that we are clueless and just can't predict the long-term consequences of our actions (see Chapter 3; Greaves, 2016; Lenman, 2000). Against this, many effective altruists argue that the risk of an existential disaster gives us an opportunity to affect the long-term future in expectation. As we saw, Toby Ord (2020) estimates that there is a 1 in 6 chance of an existential catastrophe in this century—and if that were to occur, then the value of the future could shrink drastically. Hence, that estimate suggests that insofar as it's possible to reduce the risk of an existential disaster this century, it could be possible to increase the expected value of the future (see Chapter 3).

Many longtermist effective altruists thus focus on reducing existential risk, paying special attention to risks from synthetic viruses and artificial intelligence (AI). Future synthetic viruses could be engineered to be maximally lethal, meaning they could be much more dangerous than viruses that aren't the result of human design (Ord, 2020). Researchers study what can be done to prevent such engineered pandemics.

Similarly, AI systems are growing more powerful every year, and an increasing number of experts worry that they could pose a risk to humanity (Bostrom, 2014; Center for AI Safety, 2023; Ord, 2020; Russell, 2019). While there are still many things AI systems cannot do, many longtermists believe that their capabilities will eventually surpass those of humans and that they then could cause great harm—either by mistake or by conscious design. To prevent that, many effective altruists research risks from advanced AI.

But while existential risk reduction is the most popular strategy to affect the long-term future, it is not the only one. In his recent book *What We Owe the Future*, William MacAskill (2022) discusses a range of other interventions, including researching better strategies for doing good and spreading values. But since those interventions are not uniquely tied to longtermism but are more general in nature, we discuss them separately.

Meta Causes

As we saw in Chapter 5, people often prefer to help others directly and can be suspicious of indirect forms of doing good. However, effective altruists don't share that view. They are happy to do good in more indirect or "meta" ways, as long as it is effective.

One meta-strategy is *global priorities research*: researching new causes and key considerations that may affect our estimates of the effectiveness of existing causes. It's possible that there are causes that have even higher impact than the ones effective altruists currently focus on, meaning that finding them would allow huge amounts of resources to be allocated more effectively. Therefore, global priorities research could itself be highly effective. For such reasons, many effective altruists pursue global priorities research.

Another meta-strategy is spreading the ideas and values of effective altruism. As we saw in Chapter 5, that can have a large so-called multiplier effect. People who introduce others to effective altruism can thereby increase their impact if those new people go on to have a substantial impact of their own. Building on such reasoning, many effective altruists work on outreach and movement-building, for example, at the Centre for Effective Altruism. Thanks in part to these efforts, the effective altruism movement had an estimated 7400 engaged members in 2021 (Todd, 2021b).

Impact Strategies

Once we have settled on a cause, the next questions are as follows: How can we contribute to this cause? What strategies should we use? How should we allocate the resources in our effective altruism budget to make progress on our chosen cause?

We can distinguish between two broad classes of strategies: using our *money* (through donations) and using our *time* (through volunteering or professional work).

Money

Effective altruism is not only cause-neutral but also *means-neutral* or *strategy-neutral*: That is, it says that we shouldn't be biased in favor of any particular strategy but should rather assess all the different strategies we could use and choose the most effective one (Effective Altruism Forum, n.d.b). While effective altruism is often associated with donations, it is not just about that. It can often be more important to use your time effectively, as we will see.

That said, donations have several advantages as a strategy for doing good. First, it's a widely available strategy since many people in the Western world can donate at least some money. Second, it is very flexible, unlike many strategies where we use our time. While it can be difficult to switch to a higher-impact job, switching your donations from one charity to another is normally straightforward and easy.

When we're thinking about donations, it's important to notice the huge range of projects they can support. A word like *charity* tends to have associations with directly providing, for example, medicine or food to poor people (cf. the direct transfer model we discussed in Chapter 5). That can certainly be a good use of money if we give them to, for example, the GiveWell-recommended global poverty charities. But donations can also support very different kinds of projects, including research, political campaigns, online infrastructure like OurWorldInData.org, and much more. We should consider all these different projects without prejudice and support the ones that we estimate to have the highest impact.

Time

Using your time to help others is, of course, a well-known strategy outside of effective altruism. It is probably mostly associated with volunteering: working for a charity, for example, a few hours a week outside of your regular job. But, as discussed in Chapter 5, effective altruists argue that such volunteering is usually less effective than alternative strategies. It's hard to be really effective at something if you only work on it a few hours a week. Instead, it is often more effective to choose a professional job that has a high impact (Todd, 2020).

Career Choice

One of the most important decisions in our lives is our choice of career. As we saw in Chapter 6, we spend about 80,000 hours—a huge part of our lives—at work; and if we use them well, we could have a tremendous impact. Just as the most effective charities are much more effective than the average charity, the most effective careers are much more effective than the average career (Todd, 2021a). Therefore, it's a decision worth investing a lot of time in.

Effective altruists recognized the importance of career choice early on, and in 2011 William MacAskill and Benjamin Todd set up 80,000 Hours to advise young people on how to choose high-impact careers (80,000 Hours, n.d.). 80,000 Hours produces a range of content on career choice, hosts a job board, and provides free coaching to people who want to pursue an altruistically motivated career. The careers that they recommend are very broad in scope and include research, grant-making, advocacy, policy, entrepreneurship, and much more. People who have already chosen a career path can also benefit from their information about different options and potential job shifts.

Voting

80,000 hours recommends many jobs and careers relating to politics and policy (Mann & Batty, 2018; Koehler, 2021; Hilton & Todd, 2023). But there are also other ways to take political action. In particular, voting can be a great way of having an impact.

At first glance, it may seem as if voting doesn't make a difference since the chance that a single vote will decide an election is small. But, more often than not, such thinking rests on poor expected value calculations or a failure to even make such calculations in the first place (Chapter 5). While it is true that the chance that your vote will be decisive is small, it does happen: For example, it did in a Virginia state vote in 2017 (Reuters, 2017). And the impact of a decisive vote could be immense. Suppose, for instance, that your vote would determine the outcome of the American presidential election. That would cause a different party to have the presidency for 4 years, which would be hugely consequential.

William MacAskill tries to quantify these effects in his book *Doing Good Better* (2015). Obviously, they are very rough estimates that depend on several assumptions (the interested reader is referred to MacAskill's book for details). However, it can still be valuable to look at these estimates—in particular since they provide an illustrative example of how useful the concept of expected value is. Suppose that one party is better than the other (by your lights), thanks to them pursuing better policies, having more competent leadership, and so on. MacAskill estimates that the value of that party winning the presidential election is $1000 per American, which equals more than $300 billion in total—a positively huge number. That means that even though the chance of your vote being decisive is small—MacAskill cites data saying it was 1 in 60 million in 2008—the expected value of voting is still big (Gelman et al., 2012). More precisely, it was more than $5000 in 2008. Such estimates suggest that voting can often be a good use of your time.

Engaging With Effective Altruist Ideas

We have only scratched the surface of the effective altruism philosophy and the specific causes that effective altruists prioritize, instead focusing on the psychology of effective altruism. There is much more to learn via the books, websites, and other resources mentioned throughout this chapter. Reading such material and learning more can be an effective activity. Counterintuitively, in the short term it can have a higher impact than doing good directly, for example, via donating to an effective charity. As we have seen, the difference in effectiveness between different strategies for improving the world is huge. That means that getting a deep understanding of the relevant considerations is crucial.

Naively one might think that to be effective in altruistic contexts, it suffices to go to an effective altruist charity evaluator's website and look at their recommendations. Such websites certainly are very useful, as we have seen (Chapter 6)—and following their advice typically greatly increases your impact. At the same time, if we really want to maximize our impact, we cannot let such recommendations wholly replace our own judgment. For one thing, effective altruist charity evaluators give partially conflicting advice. Thus, to make an informed decision about what causes to prioritize and which strategy to pursue, we must inform ourselves.

Connecting With Others Interested in Effective Altruism
Another thing that can have a much higher impact than it may seem is connecting with others who are interested in effective altruism. Talking to seasoned effective altruists can give a better understanding of effective altruist ideas. Moreover, people can be much more effective if they work together. Accordingly, the effective altruism community is intensely collaborative. Many people who want to do good divide their time into two parts: They spend most of it at their day job—whose primary function is to earn money—and then volunteer for a charity in their spare time to have an impact. By contrast, effective altruists tend to specialize in what they're best suited for. Some effective altruists focus solely on making money to give to effective charities ("earning to give"), whereas others solely work directly for those charities. Still others give advice about which career paths are best (e.g., 80,000 Hours) or work on growing the effective altruism community (e.g., the Centre for Effective Altruism). While specialization and division of labor are generally used more extensively in the for-profit world than in altruistic projects, the effective altruism community is an exception. That is a reason to connect with the effective altruism ecosystem.

Future Directions

Effective altruism has long been a neglected topic not only in the world at large but also in academia specifically. While there has been a lot of research on the psychology of altruism, only a small part of it has been focused on why altruistic behavior is frequently not particularly effective.

But in recent years, that has started to change. There has been more research on the psychology of effective altruism. In this book, we have tried to summarize that research. In Part I, we presented a theory of why altruism is often less effective than it could be. In previous chapters in Part II, we discussed what can be done to increase the effectiveness of altruistic efforts on a societal level. And in this last chapter we have provided some practical advice on what individuals can do to make their altruism more effective.

There are many ways in which future research could deepen and extend our knowledge of the psychology of effective altruism. We find the following topics particularly promising:

Develop and test interventions that increase the effectiveness of people's help. An example of such an intervention is Giving Multiplier (Chapter 6), which uses the observation that people have a preference for splitting to increase the effectiveness of their giving. No doubt, there could be other interventions of the same sort that use people's psychological tendencies to make their help more effective. More research on such interventions could be very useful.

Devise more tests of effective altruist inclinations. In Chapter 7, we presented research showing that expansive altruism and effectiveness-focus predict interest in effective altruism. While that was a useful first step, we need more research that could help us to better understand the psychological structure of enthusiasm about effective altruism. For details of potentially useful research projects, see the penultimate section of Chapter 7.

Study effective altruist value change. As we saw in Chapter 8, there has been a relatively limited amount of research on fundamental value change that is relevant to effective altruism. New research could teach us about, for instance, what the effects of rational arguments and norm changes might be. Relatedly, more research on what demographic groups are most positively disposed to the effective altruist message would be useful.

Study the psychology of non-donation strategies for doing good. Most research on the psychology of effective altruism is focused on charitable giving. As discussed in the Introduction, this is understandable since it is often much more methodologically straightforward to study one-off giving decisions than to study long-term altruistic efforts, like impact-oriented careers. Studies of such strategies may need to be conducted over multiple years (e.g., to follow career progression) and will, no doubt, typically be more time-intensive. Nevertheless, such studies could be worthwhile.

Study cross-cultural differences. With few exceptions, research on the effectiveness of altruistic efforts doesn't consider cross-cultural differences (Kogut et al., 2015). Instead, most studies focus on developed countries in North America and Europe. We need more research examining the extent to which those studies generalize globally. Researchers could take well-known studies and try to replicate them in new countries.

Study the psychology of particular high-impact causes, such as the long-term future or animal welfare. In this book, we've mostly discussed *cause-general* strategies for increasing the effectiveness of people's help: strategies that are not tied to any specific cause but rather make people's help more effective in general. But there are also *cause-specific strategies*, which identify particular high-impact causes, such as the long-term future or animal welfare, and try to increase the resources going toward them. More psychological research on interventions related to specific high-impact causes would be useful.

Concluding Words

Most people want to do good and are willing to make sacrifices to help others. Cynics argue that humans are selfish, but to the contrary, all over the world people display striking levels of altruism. They donate to charity, volunteer, and even choose careers with the aim of helping worse-off people. But unfortunately, much of their help is far less effective than it could be. That means that all this altruism doesn't translate into nearly as much real-world impact as one would have wanted.

In this book, we've shown why that is. Effective altruism doesn't come naturally to most people. Many psychological obstacles stand in its way, including the norm that we should help based on our feelings even if it reduces effectiveness (Chapter 1), insensitivity to the big differences in effectiveness across altruistic interventions (Chapter 2), neglect of distant beneficiaries (Chapter 3), aversion to deprioritizing less effective interventions (Chapter 4), and misconceptions about the concept of effectiveness (Chapter 5). But while it can be difficult to overcome these obstacles, it is not impossible. We can address them by simple nudges and incentive systems (Chapter 6) but also by teaching people about the philosophy of effective altruism (Chapter 8). Initially, effective altruism may primarily appeal to those who find its core principles intuitive (Chapter 7), but with time larger groups may come to adopt them via changing norms.

The growth of the effective altruism movement shows that the obstacles to effective altruism aren't insurmountable. Some people have demonstrably become more effective at doing good. An important task for psychological research is to understand the obstacles to effective altruism and the best strategies for overcoming them. We have tried to take a first step.

References

Albert Schweitzer Foundation. (2020, December 10). *Burger King says no to cage eggs worldwide*. https://albertschweitzerfoundation.org/news/burger-king-says-no-to-cage-eggs-worldwide

Anderson, J. (2018). *Giving to animals: New data on who and how*. Faunalytics. Retrieved January 29, 2024 from https://faunalytics.org/giving-to-animals-new-data-who-how/#

Animal Charity Evaluators. (2024, January). *Why farmed animals?* https://animalcharityevaluators.org/donation-advice/why-farmed-animals/. Retrieved January 15, 2024.

Animal Charity Evaluators. (n.d.). *Recommended charities*. Retrieved January 15, 2024. https://animalcharityevaluators.org/donation-advice/recommended-charities/

Banker, S. (2016, September 5). McDonald's risky commitment to a cage free eggs supply chain. *Forbes*. https://www.forbes.com/sites/stevebanker/2016/09/05/mcdonalds-risky-commitment-to-a-cage-free-eggs-supply-chain/?sh=5d62ec155e3f

Bazerman, M. H. (2020). *Better, not perfect: A realist's guide to maximum sustainable goodness*. HarperCollins.

Berger, A. (2023, May 10). *Our progress in 2022 and plans for 2023*. https://www.openphilanthropy.org/research/our-progress-in-2022-and-plans-for-2023/

Bostrom, N. (2014). *Superintelligence: Paths, dangers, strategies*. Oxford University Press.

Center for AI Safety. (2023). *Statement on AI risk*. https://www.safe.ai/statement-on-ai-risk

The Centre for Effective Altruism. (2023, October). *Introduction to effective altruism program syllabus*. https://docs.google.com/document/d/1ju83W3yFqvUBvsSrHadjEwazNBphCTmLWd-xZkVArBM/edit. Retrieved February 1, 2024.

Duda, R. (2023, June). *Global priorities research*. 80,000 Hours. https://80000hours.org/problem-profiles/global-priorities-research/. Retrieved January 15, 2024.

Effective Altruism Forum. (n.d.a). *Ethics of personal consumption*. Retrieved January 27, 2024, from https://forum.effectivealtruism.org/topics/ethics-of-personal-consumption

Effective Altruism Forum. (n.d.b). *Means neutrality*. Retrieved Retrieved January 27, 2024 from https://forum.effectivealtruism.org/topics/means-neutrality.

80,000 Hours. (n.d.). *About us: what do we do, and how can we help?* Retrieved January 27, 2024, from https://80000hours.org/about/

Fountain, H. (2013, May 12). Building a $325,000 burger. *New York Times.* https://www.nytimes.com/2013/05/14/science/engineering-the-325000-in-vitro-burger.html

Galef, J. (2020, August 9). *A pretty-good mathematical model of perfectionism*. https://jessegalef.com/2020/08/09/a-pretty-good-mathematical-model-of-perfectionism/

Gelman, A., Silver, N., & Edlin, A. (2012). What is the probability your vote will make a difference? *Economic Inquiry*, *50*(2), 321–326.

GiveWell. (2023a, July). *Cost-effectiveness* https://www.givewell.org/how-we-work/our-criteria/cost-effectiveness. Retrieved January 29, 2024.

GiveWell. (2023b, July). *Our top charities*. https://www.givewell.org/charities/top-charities. Retrieved January 29, 2024.

Global Philanthropy Tracker (2023). Lilly Family School of Philanthropy. https://scholarworks.iupui.edu/server/api/core/bitstreams/09eba67a-185b-4f3c-ab40-3869ee430079/content

Good Food Institute. (n.d.). *The science of cultivated meat*. Retrieved February 1, 2024, from https://gfi.org/science/the-science-of-cultivated-meat/

Greaves, H. (2016). Cluelessness. *Proceedings of the Aristotelian Society*, *116*(3), 311–339.

Greaves, H., & MacAskill, W. (2021). *The case for strong longtermism* (No. 5-2021). Global Priorities Institute. https://globalprioritiesinstitute.org/wp-content/uploads/The-Case-for-Strong-Longtermism-GPI-Working-Paper-June-2021-2-2.pdf

Greaves, H., MacAskill, W., O'Keeffe-O'Donovan, R., Trammell, P., Tereick, B., Mogensen, A., Tarsney, C., Alexandrie, G., de Sévricourt, M. C., Aung, J., Bruckamp, L., Mori, J., Pomarius, L., & Herrmann, S. (2020). *A research agenda for the Global Priorities Institute* (No. 2.1). Global Priorities Institute. https://globalprioritiesinstitute.org/wp-content/uploads/GPI-research-agenda-version-2.1.pdf

Hillebrandt, H., & Halstead, J. G. (2020, January 16). *Growth and the case against randomista development*. Effective Altruism Forum. https://forum.effectivealtruism.org/posts/bsE5t6qhGC65fEpzN/growth-and-the-case-against-randomista-development

Hilton, B. & Todd, B. (2023, December 14). *Policy and political skills*. 80,000 Hours. https://80000hours.org/skills/political-bureaucratic/. Retrieved January 29, 2024.

Koehler, A. (October, 2021). *Policy careers focused on other pressing global issues*. 80,000 Hours. Retrieved February 1, 2024, from https://80000hours.org/career-reviews/policy-careers-focused-on-other-pressing-global-issues/

Kogut, T., Slovic, P., & Västfjäll, D. (2015). Scope insensitivity in helping decisions: Is it a matter of culture and values?. *Journal of Experimental Psychology: General*, *144*(6), 1042–1052.

Layard, R., & Oparina, E. (2021). Living long and living well: The WELLBY approach. In J. F. Helliwell, R. Layard, J. D. Sachs, & J. E. D. Neve (Eds.), *World happiness report* (pp. 191–208). Sustainable Development Solutions Network.

Lenman, J. (2000). Consequentialism and cluelessness. *Philosophy & Public Affairs*, *29*(4), 342–370.

MacAskill, W. (2015). *Doing good better: Effective altruism and a radical new way to make a difference*. Guardian Faber Publishing.

MacAskill, W. (2022). *What we owe the future: A million-year view*. Oneworld Publications.

MacAskill, W., Meissner, D., & Chappell, R.Y. (2023). *The rights objection*. Utilitarianism. https://www.utilitarianism.net/objections-to-utilitarianism/rights. Retrieved January 29, 2024.

Mann, A., & Batty, R. (2018, May). *Congressional staffer*. 80,000 Hours. https://80000hours.org/career-reviews/congressional-staffer/. Retrieved January 29, 2024.

Nielsen, M. (2022, June 3). *Notes on effective altruism*. Michael's Notebook. https://michaelnotebook.com/eanotes/

Ord, T. (2020). *The precipice: Existential risk and the future of humanity*. Hachette Books.

Pritchett, L. (2020). Randomizing development: Method or Madness. In F. Bédécarrats, I. Guérin, and F. Roubaud, (Eds.), *Randomized control trials in the field of development, a critical perspective* (pp. 79–107). Oxford University Press.

Railton, P. (1984). Alienation, consequentialism, and the demands of morality. *Philosophy & Public Affairs*, *13*(2), 134–171.

Reuters (2017, December 20). *Democrat wins by one vote in Virginia legislative election recount*. https://www.reuters.com/article/us-usa-politics-virginia-idUSKBN1ED2XQ

Russell, S. J. (2019). *Human compatible: Artificial intelligence and the problem of control*. Viking.

Schubert, S., & Caviola, L. (2023). Virtues for real-world utilitarians. In H. Viciana, A. Gaitán, & F. A. González (Eds.), *Experiments in moral and political philosophy* (pp. 163–184). Routledge.

Singer, P. (1972). Famine, affluence, and morality. *Philosophy and Public Affairs*, *3*(1), 229–243.

Singer, P. (2015). *The most good you can do: How effective altruism is changing ideas about living ethically*. Yale University Press.

Sobel, D. (2020). *Understanding the demandingness objection*. Oxford University Press.

Tanyi, A., & Bruder, M. (2014). Consequentialism and its demands: A representative study. *The Journal of Value Inquiry*, *48*(2), 293–314.

Thomas, J. (2023). *The farm animal movement: Effective altruism, venture philanthropy, and the fight to end factory farming in America*. Lantern Publishing & Media.

Timmerman, T., & Cohen, Y. (2019, May 20). Actualism and possibilism in ethics. In E. N. Zalta (Ed.), *Stanford encyclopedia of philosophy* (Fall 2020 ed.). https://plato.stanford.edu/entries/actualism-possibilism-ethics/

Todd, B. (2020, December). *Where's the best place to volunteer?* 80,000 Hours. https://80000hours.org/articles/volunteering/. Retrieved January 27, 2024.

Todd, B. (2021a, September). *The best solutions are far more effective than others*. 80,000 Hours. https://80000hours.org/articles/solutions/. Retrieved January 15, 2024.

Todd, B. (2021b, July 28). Is effective altruism growing? An update on the stock of funding vs people. *80,000 Hours*. https://80000hours.org/2021/07/effective-altruism-growing/. Retrieved January 15, 2024.

Wiblin, R. (2019, October). *A framework for comparing global problems in terms of expected impact*. 80,000 Hours. https://80000hours.org/articles/problem-framework/. Retrieved January 15, 2024.

Wiblin, R., & Harris, K. (2021, February 15). *Lewis Bollard on big wins against factory farming and how they happened*. The 80,000 Hours Podcast. https://80000hours.org/podcast/episodes/lewis-bollard-big-wins-against-factory-farming/

Williams, B. (1985). *Ethics and the limits of philosophy*. Fontana.
Wise, J. (2015, October 22). Burnout and self-care. *Giving Gladly* (blog). http://www.givinggladly.com/2015/10/burnout-and-self-care.html
Wolf, S. (1982). Moral saints. *The Journal of Philosophy*, *79*(8), 419–439.
World Bank. (2023, October 17). *Poverty*. https://www.worldbank.org/en/topic/poverty/overview. Retrieved January 13, 2024.
Yudkowsky, E. (2009, April 1). *Purchase fuzzies and utilons separately*. LessWrong. https://www.lesswrong.com/posts/3p3CYauiX8oLjmwRF/purchase-fuzzies-and-utilons-separately

Acknowledgments

This book has been long in the making. Much of our empirical work on psychological obstacles to effective altruism was conducted at the Oxford Social Behavioural and Ethics Lab, led by Nadira Faber (who also was Lucius's DPhil supervisor). Nadira was extremely helpful and generous, giving us freedom to explore as well as crucial support. We owe her our deep-felt gratitude. We also want to thank our other collaborators, including Julian Savulescu (Lucius's co-supervisor), Joshua Greene (Lucius's postdoc supervisor at Harvard), David Althaus, Jim Everett, Spencer Greenberg, Guy Kahane, Joshua Lewis, Maximilian Maier, Andreas Mogensen, David Moss, Jason Nemirow, Fabienne Sandkühler, Elliot Teperman, and Matti Wilks. We are grateful to Bryan Roberts, Mehrun Absar, and Laura O'Keefe at the Centre for Philosophy of Natural and Social Science at the London School of Economics and Political Science and Deborah Sheehan, Rocci Wilkinson, and Miriam Wood at the Oxford Uehiro Centre for Practical Ethics, all of whom provided key logistical support without which we could not have written this book. And Anne-Marie Nussberger was a great friend and companion to have at the Oxford SoBE Lab.

We thank Erin Morrissey, who provided excellent help with the preparation of the manuscript. She gave many well-judged suggestions and did much to improve the language. We also thank the many people who gave helpful comments on our drafts, including, Tom Adamczewski, Carter Allen, Adam Bales, Max Bazerman, Adam Bear, Harri Besceli, Drew Carton, Matt Coleman, Simon Eckerström Liedholm, Ben Garfinkel, Ben Grodeck, John Halstead, Mats Johansson, Samantha Kassirer, Joshua Lewis, Maximilian Maier, George Rosenfeld, Sebastian Schmidt, Philipp Schoenegger, Göran Schubert, Magdalena Schubert, Pablo Stafforini, Caj Strandberg, Jessie Sun, and David Westlund. We're also grateful for the many constructive comments from the anonymous reviewers, which clearly improved the book. And we're grateful to Emil Wasteson, Kiryl Shantyka, and everyone else at Effective Altruism Sweden for their kind help. We thank Luke Ding for his support, and Effective Ventures Foundation and Open Philanthropy for funding our research. Finally, we thank Nadina Persaud, Sarah Ebel, and the rest of the team at Oxford University Press, who were very helpful throughout this journey.

Index

For the benefit of digital users, indexed terms that span two pages (e.g., 52–53) may, on occasion, appear on only one of those pages.

Figures are indicated by *f* following the page number.

actively open-minded thinking, 129–30
Against Malaria Foundation, 15, 113, 156–57
AI (artificial intelligence), 51, 159
aid response, 40*f*, 40
AIDS interventions, 34
Althaus, David, 51, 121
altruism
    cause-general strategies, 165
    cause-specific strategies, 165
    effectiveness gap, 92–95
    emotional helping, 17–19
    expansive, 5–6, 121–25, 128
    nearsighted, 44–60
    non-donation strategies, 3–4, 165
    toward distant causes, 44–60
altruistic decision-making. *See* decision-making
Animal Charity Evaluators, 13–14, 105, 157–58
animals
    altruism toward, 55
    pet speciesism, 55–56
animal welfare
    as highest-impact cause, 157–58
    psychology of, 165
animal welfare charities
    donations directed toward, 13–14, 52–53
    recommended charities, 13–14
anthropocentric speciesism, 53–54, 55–56
arguments
    emotion-based, 140
    interactions with norms, 142–45
    moral, 135–42
    reason-based, 135, 137, 140, 142

arthritis charities, 84, 86, 139–40
arthritis research, 12, 13, 16, 17–18, 25–26, 72–73
artificial intelligence (AI), 51, 159
aversion to risky giving, 68, 90–92
aversion to waste, 25–26, 81

Baby Jessica, 38
Bastian, Brock, 53
Bazerman, Max, 47, 139, 149
BBB Wise Giving Alliance, 77–78
behavioral contagion, 144
Behavioural Insights Team (Nudge Unit), 106–7
Bergh, Robin, 102–3
Bloom, Paul, 55
bundling donations, 107–11, 153–54
Burger King, 157–58
Burum, Bethany, 24

cancer
    charities, 13, 73, 84, 86–87, 139–40
    interventions against, 34, 72
    research, 12, 13, 16, 17–18, 25–26, 72–73
career choices, 4, 32, 95, 101, 106, 123, 124, 127, 161–62, 165
Carroll, Sean, 114
CART (Comprehensive Assessment of Rational Thinking), 130–31
cataract surgery, 33
cause-general strategies, 165
cause-neutrality, 14, 150, 155
causes
    deprioritizing, 5, 61–62
    distant, 44–60
    highest-impact, 155–60

causes (*cont.*)
    prioritizing (*see* prioritizing)
    psychology of, 44–60, 165
cause-specific strategies, 165
Caviola, Lucius, 48, 51, 54, 55, 79–80, 82, 107, 124–25
Centre for Effective Altruism, 160
character, evidence of, 23–24, 110
charitable giving, 4. *See also* donations; giving
    based on personal connections, 13–14
    based on urgency, 14–15
    cost-effectiveness estimates of, 24, 30–31
    direct vs indirect impact of, 82–84
    effectiveness gap, 92–95
    emotional helping, 17–19
    failure to research before, 16–17
    market for, 34–36
    norms of, 11–29
    obligations to donate effectively, 22–23
    parochialism in, 44–47
    presentism in, 44, 47–52
    risky, 90–92
    speciesism in, 44, 52–56
    subjective approach to, 4, 11, 12
    as supererogatory, 20
charities. *See also* causes
    animal, 13–14
    comparability of, 84–85, 88–90
    cross-cause comparability, 24, 88–90
    disaster relief, 14–15
    effectiveness of (*see* effectiveness)
    funding gaps, 68
    global poverty, 31, 41, 46–47
    insensitivity to scale, 36–38
    loyalty to, 14
    market inefficiency, 34–36
    meta-charities, 83–84
    overhead costs, 32–33, 76–81
    recommended, 13–14, 15, 105–6, 113, 117, 156–58
    terminology for, 1, 161
charity evaluators, 83–84
Charity Navigator, 77–78
Charity Watch, 77–78
children
    drowning child argument, 20–21, 62, 136

speciesism, 55
choice architecture, 106–7
circle of moral concern, 46
Clean Air Task Force, 113
Clinton, Hillary, 144
cluelessness, 52
cognitive misers, 129
Cokelet, Bradford, 140–41
collaborativeness, 131
Compassion in World Faming USA, 13–14
Comprehensive Assessment of Rational Thinking (CART), 130–31
conformity bias, 19
connecting with others, 163
consumption decisions, 1, 16, 21–22, 35–36, 48, 64, 65, 77, 92–95, 106
corporate campaigns, 13–14
cost-effectiveness
    definition of, 1, 30, 33–34, 84–88
    evaluation of, 79, 85
    of global health interventions, 34, 35f
cost-effectiveness estimates of global poverty charities, 30–31
    Cost per life ratio version, 30–31
    Explicit comparison version, 30–31
    Tipping point version, 30–31
Cost per life ratio (method for estimating the cost-effectiveness of global poverty charities), 30–31
cultivated meat, 158
cultural evolution, 144–45
Cushman, Fiery, 137
cynical theory of helping behavior, 2, 19

decision-making, 11–12
    objective approach to, 11
    subjective approach to, 11, 16–17
    two-budget strategy for, 149–51
demographic correlations, 124, 127–28
deprioritizing causes, 5, 61–62
determination, 131
Deworm the World Initiative, 107, 113
Dhont, Kristof, 54
Dickert, Stephan, 40
disaster relief, 14–15
    aid response as function of number of, 40f, 40

distant causes, 44–60
donations. *See also* charitable giving
   advantages for doing good, 160–61
   annual US, 1
   bundling, 107–11, 153–54
   donor coordination, 114–17
   as an impact strategy, 160–61
   matching, 111–12, 114–17
   micro-matching, 114–17
   prioritizing causes to give to (*see* prioritizing)
   splitting, 67–71
drowning child argument, 20–21, 62, 136

educational interventions, 34
effective altruism
   cause-general strategies for, 165
   cause-specific strategies for, 165
   connecting with others interested in, 163
   definition of, 1, 3, 84–88, 122–23, 129
   engaging with, 162–63
   enthusiasts, 120–34
   future directions for psychological research on, 164–65
   impact strategies, 160–63
   interventions for overcoming obstacles to (*see* interventions)
   introductions to, 4, 155
   for mortals, 149, 165–66
   as a normative framework, 3
   obligations for, 22–23
   obstacles to (*see* obstacles)
   social incentives for, 23–25
   tough prioritizing for, 61–63, 74
   two-budget strategy for, 149–51
   ways to practice, 3–4
effective altruism enthusiasts, finding, 120–21, 132
effective altruist value change, 135–48, 164
effective altruist virtues, 154–55
effective charities, 1, 4–5, 16–17, 30–32, 68, 113, 156–58
effectiveness
   determinants of, 32–33, 76–77

   failure to research, 16–17
   insensitivity to scale, 36–38
   as a key criterion in charitable giving, 25–26
   measurement of, 30, 84–88
   misconceptions about, 76–98
   of moral arguments, 137–41
   of splitting donations, 67–71
effectiveness differences, 30, 31–32, 41–42
   effects on donations, 38
   estimation of, 30–32
   vast, 32–34
effectiveness-focus, 5–6, 121–22, 125–28
effectiveness-focus scale, 126–27
effectiveness gap, 92–95
80,000 Hours (website), 4, 106, 161–62
Elmore, Holly, 63
emergencies, 14–15, 62
emotional arguments, 140
emotional helping
   nearsighted altruism, 44, 56–57
   norm of, 17–19
   uncorrelated with effectiveness, 19
Enlightenment: The, 144
environmental charities, 52–53
ethics classes, 140–41
evaluation of interventions and charities (by laypeople)
   joint, 38, 40, 64, 79, 80, 112
   separate, 37–38, 64, 79, 80, 112
Everett, Jim, 54
Evidence Action, 107, 113
evidence of character, 23–24, 110
existential risk, 50–51, 52, 158–59
expansive altruism, 5–6, 121–25, 128
expansive altruism scale, 123–24
expected value, 90–91
expected WELLBYs, 90
expert recommendations as a strategy to increase the effectiveness of people's help, 104–6
Explicit comparison of charities (method for estimating the cost-effectiveness of global poverty charities), 30–31
externalities, 93–95
extinction, human, 3–4, 49–51

Faber, Nadira, 30–31, 49–50, 53, 54

fairness, 71–73
favorite-effective bundles, 109–10, 111–12
feelings, nearsighted, 44, 56–57
Founders Pledge, 13–14, 105
Frank, Robert H., 144
funding gaps, 68
fundraising charities, 83
future, long-term
    as highest-impact cause, 52, 158–59
    psychology of, 47–52, 165
Future Meat Technologies, 158
future research on the psychology of effective altruism, 131–32, 164–65

Galef, Julia, 129
Geiser, Amanda, 48
Give Directly, 113, 139
GiveWell, 15, 46–47, 83–84, 102, 104–5, 106, 117, 157
giving. *See also* charitable giving
    based on personal connections, 13–14
    emotional helping, 17–19
    norms of, 11–12, 26–27
    social incentives for, 23–25
    voluntary, 20–22
Giving Multiplier, 112–15, 116–17, 153–54, 164
    Bill & Melinda Gates Foundation, 114
Giving What We Can, 46–47, 83, 114, 130, 136
Giving What We Can Pledge, 150–51
global health interventions, 34, 35f, 156–57
global poverty and health
    as highest-impact cause, 156–57
global poverty charities, 31, 41, 46–47, 154–55
Global Priorities Institute (University of Oxford), 156
global priorities research, 156, 159–60
Gneezy, Ayelet, 103–4, 111
Gneezy, Uri, 111
Good Food Institute, 113, 158
Goodwin, Geoffrey, 51
Greenberg, Spencer, 30–31
Greene, Joshua, 47, 107, 139, 140
Grodeck, Ben, 138–39
guide dogs, 33

GuideStar, 77–78

Haidt, Jonathan, 137
half-measure strategy, 151–54, 153f
Happiness Lab podcast, 114
Haran, Uriel, 130
Harris, Sam, 114
Hassenfeld, Elie, 104–5
health interventions
    cost-effectiveness of, 34, 35f
    evaluation of, 86–88
    global poverty and health, 156–57
    quality-adjusted life years (QALYs) metric, 33–34, 85–86, 86f, 94
    well-being-adjusted life years (WELLBYs), 86–88, 90, 94, 155
heavy tails, 34, 35f
highest-impact causes, 155–60
High Impact Athletes, 83
Hoffman, Moshe, 24
homophobia, 54
Horton, Joe, 25, 136
Huang, Karen, 47, 139
human extinction, 3–4, 49–51
Humane League, 113
The Humane League, 13–14, 157–58
humanitarian catastrophes, 37

idealistic theory of helping behavior, 2
identifiable victims, 38–39
IDEO, 114
ignorance, veil of, 47, 73
impact strategies, 160–63
incentives, 101, 117
    social, 23–25
    through donation matching, 111–12
inefficiency, market, 34–36
information
    providing, to dispel misconceptions about effective altruism, 101–6, 117
    veil of ignorance, 47, 73, 139
interventions to increase the effectiveness of people's help
    arguments and norms together, 142–45
    avoiding the half-measure fallacy, 151–54, 153f
    development of, 164
    effective altruist virtues, 154–55

expert recommendations, 104–6
finding enthusiasts, 120–21, 132
fundamental value change, 135–42, 145
information, nudges, and incentives, 101–12, 117
moral arguments, 135–48
two-budget strategy, 149–54, 153f
investment decisions (for personal gain), 1, 11–12, 16, 17–18, 30, 36, 67–71, 77, 84, 90, 92–95

Jessica (Baby), 38
Johns Hopkins Center for Health Security, 113
joint evaluation, 38, 40, 64, 79, 80, 112

Kahane, Guy, 53, 55
Kahneman, Daniel, 37
Kant, Immanuel, 70
Kantian fallacy, 70
Kaposi's sarcoma, 34
Karlan, Dean, 102–3
Karnofsky, Holden, 104–5
Keenan, Elizabeth, 103–4, 111
Helen Keller International, 15, 113, 157
Knetsch, Jack, 37
Kuhn, Fabio, 112–13

Lewis, Joshua, 48, 82, 121, 124–25
The Life You Can Save, 83
Lindauer, Matthew, 138, 140
long-term future
    as highest-impact cause, 52, 158–59
    psychology of, 47–52, 165
longtermism, 52, 159
Los Angeles Times, 114
loyalty, 14

MacAskill, William, 4, 61–62, 129, 155, 157, 159, 161–62
malaria, 20, 34, 38–39, 73, 86
Malaria Consortium, 15
malaria mitigation charities, 15, 139–40
marginal value/benefits/utility, diminishing, 39, 40f, 67–68, 69–70, 71, 87, 90, 109–10
marketing, targeted, 120–21
MarketWatch, 114

matching donations, 111–12
    micro-matching, 114–17
Mayorga, Marcus, 140
McDonald's, 157–58
means-neutrality, 160
media coverage, 38–39
medical interventions, 85–86. See also health interventions
Mellers, Barbara A., 130
meta causes, 159–60
meta-charities, 83–84
micro-matching, 114–17
Mindscape podcast, 114
misconceptions about effectiveness, 76–98
    providing information to dispel, 101–6
    related to comparing different causes, 84–90
    related to indirect impact, 82–84
    related to overhead costs, 76–81
    related to risky giving, 90–92
Mogensen, Andreas, 51
money as an impact strategy, 160–61. See also donations
moral arguments, 135–48
moral circle, 46, 122–23
moral expansiveness, 123
moral factors, 121–28
Morrisey, Erin, 124–25
Moss, David, 30–31
motivated reasoning, 53–54, 82, 129
multiplier effects, 83, 160

nearsighted altruism, 5, 44–60
Nemirow, Jason, 14–15, 77, 102
New Incentives, 113
non-donation strategies, 3–4, 165
nonprofits. See also charities
    starvation cycle, 81
    terminology for, 1
norm cascades, 143
norms
    of emotional helping, 17–19
    interactions with arguments, 142–45
    parochialist, 45
Nowak, Martin, 24
Nudge Unit (Behavioural Insights Team), 106–7
nudging, 101, 106–11, 117

Obama, Barack, 144
objective approach to decision-making, 11
obligatory actions, 20, 22–23
obstacles to effective altruism
    aversion to deprioritization, 61–63, 74
    emotional helping, 17–19
    failure to research effectiveness, 16–17
    interventions for overcoming (*see* interventions)
    misconceptions about effectiveness, 76–98
    nearsightedness, 44–60
    neglecting the stakes, 30–43
    norms of giving, 11–12, 26–27
    opportunity cost neglect, 63–65
    taboo trade-offs, 65–67
open-minded thinking, 129–30
Open Philanthropy, 156
opportunity cost neglect, 63–65
Ord, Toby, 51, 158–59
OurWorldInData.org, 161
overhead costs, 32–33, 76–81
    aversion to, 81, 103–4
overhead myth, 76–81

Pareto efficiency, 25–26
Parfit, Derek, 25, 39–40, 49–50, 136
parochialism, 44–47
peer effects, 143
peer pressure, 144
person-affecting view, 51
personal connections, 13–14
    loyalty, 14
    vicarious, 14
pet speciesism, 55–56
philanthropy, (*see* charitable giving; donations)
plant-based alternatives to animal products, 113, 158
policy, 157–58, 161–62
poverty and health, global, 46–47, 156–57
poverty charities, 31, 41, 46–47, 113, 156–57
presentism, 44, 47–52
prioritizing, 4, 44, 56–57, 89, 155–60
    choosing humans over animals, 53–54, 55
    global priorities research, 156, 159–60

how every life matters equally, 39–40
psychological mechanisms that underpin resistance to, 61–75
Project Syndicate, 114
psychology
    of emergencies vs non-emergencies, 14–15, 62
    of high-impact causes, 44–60, 165
    of non-donation strategies, 165
Pummer, Theron, 22–23, 136

quality-adjusted life years (QALYs), 33–34, 85–86, 86*f*, 94

Rachels, James, 140–41
racism, 54, 72
Reinstein, David, 102–3
reputation, 18, 19, 23, 24, 110
resource allocation, 73
    aid response as function of number of victims, 40*f*, 40
    half-measure strategy, 151–54, 153*f*
    two-budget strategy for, 149–54, 153*f*
responsibility for outcomes, 20–22
risky giving: aversion to, 68, 90–92
Ritov, Ilana, 130
Rust, Joshua, 137
Rütheman, Daniel, 112–13

sacred values, 65–67
salience, 13, 14–15, 39–40, 46, 49–51, 61–62, 63, 64–65, 81, 111, 145
Santos, Laurie, 114
save more lives principle, 139–40
scale insensitivity, 36–38
scale-tractability-neglectedness framework, 155–56
Schoenegger, Philipp, 138–39
Schroeder, Juliana, 72
Schwitzgebel, Eric, 137, 140–41
Scientific Revolution, 144
scope insensitivity, 36–38
scope neglect, 36–38
Scout Mindset, 129
secular values, 65
separate evaluation, 37–38, 64, 79, 80, 112
sexism, 54, 72
Sharps, Daron, 72

Singer, Peter, 4, 20–21, 22, 46, 52–53, 55–56, 83, 122–23, 136, 138, 140–41
Slovic, Paul, 140
social dominance orientation, 54
social incentives, 23–25
social norms. *See* norms
social temporal discount rate, 48
Soldier Mindset, 129
species-absolutism, 55
speciesism, 44, 52–56
    anthropocentric, 53–54, 55–56
    pet, 55–56
species-relativism, 54–55
splitting donations, 67–71, 107–11, 151–54
Stanovich, Keith, 130–31
statistical victims, 38–40
subjective approach to decision-making, 11, 16–17
Sunstein, Cass, 106–7
supererogatory actions, 20
surgery, cataract, 33

Talmud, 41
targeted marketing, 120–21
temporal discount rate, 48
Teperman, Elliot, 30–31
terminology, 1, 161
testing effective altruist inclinations, 120–34, 164
Tetlock, Philip, 65–66
Thaler, Richard, 106–7
time: use of, 161–63
Tipping point (method for estimating the cost-effectiveness of global poverty charities), 30–31
Todd, Benjamin, 155, 161–62

Toplak, Maggie, 130–31
trachoma, 33, 138
trading off values, 65–67
triage situations, 61–63, 64–65
truth-seeking, 129–31, 154
two-budget strategy, 73, 149–54, 153*f*

Ubel, Peter, 72
University of Oxford's Global Priorities Institute, 156
urgency, 14–15

value(s)
    fundamental change, 135–48
    sacred, 65–67
    secular, 65
    trading off, 65–67
Västfjäll, Daniel, 140
veil of ignorance, 47, 73, 139
vicarious personal connections, 14
victims, 39
    aid response as function of number of, 40*f*, 40
    identifiable vs statistical, 38–40
virtues, effective altruist, 154–55
vitamin A deficiency charities, 15
volunteering, 1, 20, 83, 151, 161, 163
voting, 162
Vox.com, 114

Waking Up podcast, 114
waste: aversion to, 25–26, 81
well-being-adjusted life years (WELLBYs), 86–88, 90, 94, 155
West, Richard, 130–31
Wilks, Matti, 55, 130
Wood, Daniel, 102–3